PREACHING AND HOMILETICAL THEORY

Preaching and Its Partners
A series edited by Paul Scott Wilson

PREACHING AND PRACTICAL MINISTRY
Ronald J. Allen

PREACHING AND WORSHIP
Thomas H. Troeger

PREACHING AND ETHICS
Arthur Van Seters

PREACHING AND HOMILETICAL THEORY
Paul Scott Wilson

PREACHING AND
HOMILETICAL THEORY

Paul Scott Wilson

CHALICE
PRESS

ST. LOUIS, MISSOURI

Biblical quotations, unless otherwise noted, are from the *New Revised Standard Version Bible*, copyright 1989, Division of Christian Education of the National Council of the Churches of Christ in the United States of America. Used by permission. All rights reserved.

Cover art: Artville
Cover design: Michael Domínguez
Interior design: Wynn Younker
Art direction: Michael Domínguez

Visit Chalice Press on the World Wide Web at
www.chalicepress.com

10 9 8 7 6 5 4 3 2   06 07 08 09 10 11

Library of Congress Cataloging–in–Publication Data

Wilson, Paul Scott, 1949-
  Preaching and homiletical theory / Paul Scott Wilson.
    p. cm.
  Includes bibliographical references.
  ISBN-13: 978-0-827229-81-5
  ISBN-10: 0-827229-81-X (pbk. : alk. paper)
  1. Preaching. I. Title.
  BV4211.3.W55 2004
  251–dc22
                                                2004008675

Printed in the United States of America

CONTENTS

ACKNOWLEDGMENTS

This manuscript in its original form was initially conceived for the Warrack Lectures in preaching delivered in April of 2003 in Glasgow and Edinburgh. I am grateful to The Rev. Nigel Robb and the various officials of the Church of Scotland and the University of Glasgow for the privilege and generous hospitality that they extended to me on that occasion. As work progressed, other invitations enabled me to test my thoughts in a variety of venues: the E. C. Westervelt Lectures at Austin Presbyterian Theological Seminary in Austin, Texas; the Simpson Lectures at Acadia Divinity College of Acadia University in Wolfville, Nova Scotia; the Heritage Lectures at the Salvation Army Officer's Training College, St. John's, Newfoundland; and the Wardlaw Lectures in the D.Min. in Preaching Program in the Association of Chicago Theological Schools. I cannot name here all of my kind hosts who made the various experiences so rich and rewarding, but they know who they are. I extend my sincere thanks to them and to all of the individuals in various climates and seasons who helped me to clarify the thoughts expressed here, including my own doctoral and basic degree students. I thank Principal Peter Wyatt of Emmanuel College along with President Paul Gooch and the Board of Regents of Victoria University in the University of Toronto for their kindness in extending to me a half-term of sabbatical leave to do much of the research and writing. I also thank Jon Berquist for seeing the possibilities of this series on "Preaching and Its Partners" during his tenure at Chalice Press, and I thank the staff at Chalice for nurturing this particular volume to publication. Special thanks are due to Trent Butler for his insight and exceptional care in editing. I am grateful also to many colleagues in the Academy of Homiletics– in particular to John M. Rottman, Art Van Seters, Mike Rattee, and Todd Townshend–for reading the manuscript and making valuable suggestions. My greatest debt as always is to my wife, the Rev. Deanna Wilson, whose love is patient and kind and whose support enriches beyond measure my life and work.

INTRODUCTION

This book is part of a series devised to be a gentle response to critics of preaching in various theological disciplines, many of whom assume they can do little, if anything, to affect the quality of the sermons they hear. Most preachers I know work very hard at their task. Still, responsibility for good preaching lies with the entire church. The authors in this series are each asked to engage a particular theological discipline that has obvious connection to preaching, in order (1) to review the current state of that discipline, and (2) to assess the assistance it offers preachers. In other words, the purpose is to ask critically of each discipline, "Does this help preaching as much as it could?"

The subject of the present volume is, Does Homiletics Help Preaching? One layperson burst out laughing at the idea, "You might have to conclude that your job is not needed." A colleague wondered, "Where would one start?" I assume that while preaching is a gift of the Holy Spirit, it nonetheless requires knowledge and skills that can be taught. Contrary to a dominant assumption in many quarters, preaching needs not be learned *only* by doing. The purpose here is to be both appreciative and critical of homiletics. There is much to appreciate—in fact, so much that adequate appreciation cannot be expressed within the confines of these few pages. Preachers will find here a refresher course in preaching, for the main focus is upon key recent books and trends in homiletics (primarily within the last fifteen years) with a view to whether they help preachers. In addition, the aim here is to help discussion about the agenda for homiletics and preaching in the coming years.

The three sections of this book reflect the biblical, theological, and pastoral dimensions central to the homiletical task. Each section identifies a significant school of contemporary thought in addition to

1

surveying the breadth of discussion in that area. The biblical section examines the historical task of determining the setting and context of a text, as well as the hermeneutical and homiletical task as the text leads to contemporary meanings. This section highlights a new school of approach to the Bible that relies heavily, if often silently, upon reader response criticism to interpret difficult texts. The theological section deals with apprehending scripture as revelation and connecting it with established teachings of the church to determine what God is saying to the community of faith today. A dominant theological school in homiletics, though rarely acknowledged as such, is law and gospel. Here its development is traced with some surprising results. The final pastoral section deals with homiletical literature on various ethical and other issues including the nature of the congregation and the person of the preacher. A new homiletical school of radical postmodern ethics is examined along with the challenges and opportunities it represents for the pulpit.

In contrast to other volumes of this series that examine partner disciplines of preaching, this volume treats those disciplines largely from how they are represented within homiletical literature, as topics around which discussions have coalesced. Readers seeking help with specific specialized subjects (i.e., theology, the Bible, practical ministry), may be directed to the volumes in this series that deal specifically with those topics.

The Academy of Homiletics is a relatively small guild. In many ways it is an extended family, with all of the attendant positive and negative implications. Critiquing one another can be difficult because criticisms can be mistaken as personal. Holding one another accountable is part of our responsibility, however, and I hope that colleagues take the opinions expressed here as a form of both taking their work seriously and caring for the church, even as I apologize to those who do not feel their own work was given adequate or appropriate attention.

Homiletics has been taught since the early church, yet it is still young as an academic discipline in its own right, at least here in North America. Often it remains captive to the voices of those in other disciplines. It is often practiced without consensus on even basic standards for good preaching or the need for them. Homileticians have not even reached agreement on what makes a good sermon. Too often homiletics remains uncritical, treating the range of preaching possibilities as though they are equal, and appearing to be more interested in venturing possibilities than in assessing them with academic rigor. Still, as we will see in these pages, homiletics has a tremendous vibrancy and depth and has already helped to spawn a revolution in preaching in recent decades. If those who write books on preaching continue to learn better how to converse with one another in scholarly ways, the remarkable diversity and richness of the discipline will continue to grow and to demonstrate potential for both the academy and the pulpit in the century to come.

SECTION ONE

BIBLE

1

BIBLICAL PREACHING

Our starting place is the Bible. We must ask, What is biblical preaching? The obvious answer may not be adequate: Preaching is biblical when it is based on the Bible, when it uses the Bible's words, images, and stories as the basis for what it says. Most preachers strive for preaching to be biblical because the Bible is God's Word and because Christians seek to conform their lives to biblical teaching. As a church, we grant scripture authority over our lives. Good preachers understand that their role is to proclaim God's Word, not their own. The doctrines the church teaches, the sermons it preaches, and the social issues it embraces all have biblical foundations.

The Nature of Biblical Preaching

The notion that preaching is biblical when based on the Bible undergirds much preaching today. This should be a cause for celebration, but ironically it is a reason much contemporary preaching is weak. Being biblical may not be sufficient. What people find in the Bible is not necessarily what makes for excellent preaching. That is why so much time is spent in homiletics classes on exegesis, trying to ensure that historical critical tools are used effectively. At the end of such study a preacher usually has an in-depth understanding of both what the text says and what the text does not say. The preacher may not be any clearer on the preaching focus, however, if only because interpretation has become such a complicated matter.

To say that preaching is biblical when it is based on the Bible is too simple, for not all texts are equally important and not all insights into a text have equal value for preaching. Specifically, what should preachers seek to find in a biblical text to preach effective sermons? They look for the Word of God, for the word that God speaks today in and through the text, and for the encounter with the One who is the Word. They listen for a particular word that intersects with significant concrete issues in the present with disclosive and transformative power. In his *Preaching That Matters,* Stephen Farris puts the matter in terms of coherence:

> Preaching may be recognized as the word of God when it coheres with the biblical witness. Normally this will mean that the sermon will grow from our interaction with a biblical text. There are, however, textual sermons that are profoundly unbiblical and nontextual sermons that are truly biblical. The criterion is not the form of the sermon but its coherence with the biblical witness…If in preaching God speaks to us, it will in some ways be similar to the biblical witness. It will also be dissimilar in other respects, because of the passage of time and its attendant changes.[1]

In other words, preachers seek a word that both conforms to and challenges understandings the Christian community has received through tradition and experience. This word offers not only renewed understanding of who God is and who we are as God's creatures, but also–and more directly–God's present help.

A biblical text says many things. The present is a vast expanse of seemingly endless issues. God uses the preacher not to pronounce a general word to the whole world. God uses the preacher to speak a specific word to a particular congregation that has set apart this person to speak God's Word on their behalf. Since the whole text in all of its detail cannot meaningfully connect with everything, some particular aspect or aspects of the text need emphasis. In some ways choosing this point of emphasis is a small step in the sermon process, but in other ways this is the most important step a preacher can make. Thus it merits close attention here. If the Bible does not intersect with our world in an important way in the sermon, the whole thing may fall flat. Instead of having Farris's "preaching that matters," we will have the opposite.

The Thesis or Theme Sentence Approach

The standard homiletical approach, at least until recently, has been to state a thesis. This homiletical or rhetorical theory dates back to at least two centuries before Christ. Cicero in his *De Inventione* tells of Hermagoras of Temnos. Hermagoras devised a formula (or stasis) for classical rhetoric to discover what can be said about something by inventing an argument or thesis. Essentially, Hermagoras had his law students determine whether the issue at hand concerned factuality (e.g., is it true?), definition (e.g., in law, does it fit a particular definition like premeditated murder, or is it involuntary manslaughter?), or quality (e.g., is it good, necessary, or justified?). Once clear on the subject matter, the student could compose a thesis or a statement of the argument. In rhetoric, the standard rule for devising a thesis statement has been that it be a complete and declarative single sentence. Such a statement helps to ensure unity in the final speech, since a sentence has only one subject, so that a simple sentence identifies a single aspect of that subject. Moreover, every paragraph is similarly to be about one idea that serves the theme.

This notion of a thesis statement is as common as a blackboard and chalk, for the simple reason that it helps individuals to be clear about what they want to say. It can serve to prevent preachers from finding an image like "road" in a biblical text and immediately begin composing something about all the roads in life, a composition that leads over hill and dale but goes nowhere. Johann Michael Reu, whose *Homiletics* (1922) is probably the most learned homiletics text of the last century, argued that the theme must be rooted in a biblical passage and represent "the main thought of a text and not merely this or that secondary thought." In other words, "the theme is the formulated unity of the text,"[2] and the text itself may be trusted to yield one appropriate focus. Reu wrote in a period when this naïve trust had not yet been fully tested by the failure of historical criticism to yield scholarly consensus, or by literary ways of reading the Bible that raise issues of bias and perspective. His idea of the theme sentence as a kind of objective interpretation of the text's singular meaning was a traditional homiletical understanding.

Modern Perspectives on the Theme Sentence

We would have no need to review various perspectives on a theme sentence had this approach not come under recent indictment from several homiletical quarters. We may note three things from the outset: First, recent homiletical studies offer much variety in what has been said about a theme sentence. Second, what is said about a theme sentence today inevitably is about more than the sentence itself and connects to numerous larger homiletical issues, as we will see. Third, attacks on a theme sentence approach have generally assumed that the traditional view of a theme sentence still prevails and that changes and variations have been insubstantial.

THE REVOLUTION OF H. GRADY DAVIS: ORGANIC GROWTH

In his 1958 *Design for Preaching,* H. Grady Davis was most revolutionary in his idea of a sermon idea. He clearly broke with the old approach when he proposed that the sermon exhibit organic growth. The sermon was to be an idea that grows. It had to answer two questions: "What am I to talk about?"(the idea must be "narrow enough to be sharp"); and, "What does this mean/What must be said?" (the idea must have "in it a force that is expanding"). In this double-barreled way of considering a theme sentence, Davis was also breaking new ground. Most of the subsequent homiletical discussions of a theme sentence follow variations of this two-pronged approach, as we will see. He also required that the main idea be true. It should be "loaded with the realities of the human heart...life and death, courage and fear, love and hate, trust and doubt, guilt and forgiveness, pain and joy, shame, remorse, compassion, and hope." It should also be explicitly theological in that it is "one of the many facets of the gospel of Christ."[3]

HADDON ROBINSON: THE BIG IDEA

Neither Davis nor Haddon Robinson required an explicit link between the biblical text and the theme sentence. In *Biblical Preaching* Robinson employed the notion of a thesis, advocating that preachers identify a "big idea" composed of a subject and complement. The subject is always stated as a question, "What am I talking about?" The complement "'completes' the subject and asks, 'What am I saying about what I am talking about?'"[4] In formulating this pair of questions, Robinson owes an unacknowledged debt to Davis. The big idea is formed when the two are joined. For example, consider his treatment of Habakkuk 1:12–21:

> *Subject:* How could a righteous God use the evil and godless Babylon to punish a more righteous nation like Judah?
>
> *Complement:* God will also punish the Babylonians at an appointed time.

Idea: Even though God will use the wicked Babylonians to punish Judah, He will also judge the Babylonians for their sin.[5]

What guidance does Robinson offer concerning the selection of this idea? Ideas can be good or bad, he says, and only after they are clearly stated can they be evaluated for their significance; a good idea reflects reality and truth.[6]

FRED B. CRADDOCK: INDUCTIVE PREACHING

Fred B. Craddock and Thomas G. Long are explicit (1) in naming the biblical text as the source of the theme sentence, and (2) in relying on rhetoric to establish it. Craddock, whose name is synonymous with inductive and narrative preaching, more than anyone else has helped preachers move into new ways of engaging listeners. These new ways are less exclusive in appealing to more than ideas and logic. Where a deductive sermon begins with its premise and then proves it, Craddock's inductive sermon tests several possibilities and narrows to a conclusion. To accomplish this, Craddock advocates asking at the end of the exegetical process, "What is the text saying? In one sentence, and as simply as possible, state the message of the text."[7] Tom Long calls this a "focus statement."[8] Craddock's examples of focus statements (i.e., thesis sentences) often have a fresh twist, such as, "Acting like a Christian may lead to becoming one," or, "Hope can survive on almost nothing."[9] Perhaps this can be a clue for preachers wanting similar preaching freshness: let the sentence be like a paraphrase of the text in common language, much in the manner of Eugene Peterson's enormously popular fresh paraphrase of the Bible, entitled *The Message.*[10] After using Hebrew and Greek or a variety of translations to listen to the text, preachers may find it helpful to write in their own paraphrases.

To ensure that the sermon does not become too abstract or exclusively intellectual, Craddock additionally has preachers ask, "What is the text doing?" Tom Long calls this the "function statement."[11] In taking this step Craddock and Long devise their own two-pronged approach and engage a performative dimension of preaching previously seen mainly in some expressions of African American preaching. They think that the sermon should strive to produce in the congregation something of the rhetorical intent of the text, be it to correct, instruct, celebrate, probe, praise, debate, or whatever.[12] In other words, the sermon should perform the text's meaning and function. It should have both content and intent. It should be both effective and affective. For Craddock, when the sermon is doing something akin to what the text is doing, the preacher is on the right track. Long offers ecclesial direction for what preachers are locating in the Bible: "a preacher goes to a biblical text seeking to hear a word for the life of the church."[13] This rhetorical approach to sermon genesis offers at least one major advantage: from the beginning it sets the sermon in motion, not in mere abstraction, as a philosophical proposition is prone to do.

AN EXPLICITLY THEOLOGICAL APPROACH

My own approach is explicitly theological. As part of the exegetical process, I have students break the text down into many short complete sentence statements or concerns of the text. Then they select one main statement from these. This is called the major concern of the text (i.e., the theme statement), not because it is the only one possible but because it is the major one that the preacher chooses. By developing this major concern, the preacher will bring the perceived heart of the text into focus in the sermon. Concerns of the text (CT) may be found in the text itself, in relevant background information, and in commentaries and sermons on the text. Listing concerns of the text helps students to see and articulate the many ideas in a text. The text, of course, is more than a wheelbarrow full of ideas that one hauls from the Bible and dumps into this week's sermon, for texts communicate many things, including what ancient rhetoric taught: argument (*logos*), feelings (*pathos*), and character (*ethos*). Biblical texts contain images and stories, metaphors and symbols, histories and prophecies, laws and dilemmas. Still, the essential dimensions of a text for preaching are communicated most effectively with words composed into sentences or complete thoughts. Concerns of the text are like the facets of a many-sided diamond, each allowing the passage of light through the whole. Most importantly, they help the student to begin to experience the fullness of the text, to understand what is happening, to see the images, to hear the tones of voice, to feel the morning air–in short, to be there.

Most important in my understanding is that the thesis sentence, by whatever name we call it, focus on God in one of the persons of the Trinity. This meaning is what I call a "God sense" of the passage.[14] It represents one rendering of the theological heart of the text as scripture. Elizabeth Achtemeier suggested a similar God-focus in 1973.[15] I differ from her in focusing on an empowering action of God, an action of grace in or behind the text.

To distinguish it from all of the other concerns or ideas in the text, this statement is designated as the "major concern of the text" (MCT) for a particular sermon. It is expressed in a short sentence that is a complete thought, not a question or a partial sentence. It is memorable so that when repeated in the sermon, the listener hears and receives it as one possible key or entry place to the world of the preacher's meaning, the world of the gospel. This model of sermon genesis sets the sermon in motion by focusing the major concern of the text on an action of God. From God's action we discern God's nature. God's action, as opposed to some abstract attribute, also offers a means to visualize the text for effective oral communication. We may criticize some of the interpretative practices of the early church, for instance their fourfold method that sought historical, moral, eschatological, and allegorical (christological) meanings in every text, yet they were successful where we have not been, in keeping God at the center of scripture.[16] From the many concerns of a text, the preacher chooses one that focuses on God, and that gets at the heart of the text, at least for this occasion of reading.

Congregations can easily find themselves confused when preachers move from the biblical text to today because the preacher is unclear about what connection to make. To protect against this, the preacher can transpose the text's major concern into the present: "Jesus heals the woman" becomes, "Jesus heals us" or "Christ heals people today."[17] This transposed version I call the "major concern of the sermon" (MCS). The statement is hardly adequate in itself, for many Christians pray for healing but do not get it as they expect it; but this is the sermon starting to be written. The statement is nonetheless valid, and the purpose of the sermon is to witness to God's grace in authentic ways.[18]

BRYAN CHAPELL: THE FALLEN CONDITION FOCUS

Bryan Chapell also uses an explicitly theological approach for obtaining a theme sentence. He builds on the understanding that for all of the differences between the biblical situations and today, humans remain in a fallen condition. He calls this the Fallen Condition Focus of a biblical text: "The FCF is the mutual human condition that contemporary believers share with those to or for whom the text was written that requires the grace of the passage."[19] He adds, "The unifying theme of the sermon—the one thing that the message is about— is how the truths of the [biblical] passage address an FCF."[20] He seems to imply that this idea will be a statement of grace, but this is not explicitly spelled out.

THE DOUBLE-BARRELED THEME SENTENCE

Many other homileticians speak of a theme sentence in double-barreled ways. Harold T. Bryson and James C. Taylor wrote of paired terms, the "essence of the text in a sentence" and the "essence of the sermon in a sentence."[21] John Killinger, in 1985, the same year as Craddock's *Preaching,* spoke of both an idea around which the sermon is composed and a separate "statement of purpose" about what he wants to happen in people's minds. This contrasts with Craddock's and Long's emphasis on what they want people to do—a nonetheless related rhetorical thrust.[22] Also in the same year, James Cox devoted separate chapters to the "central idea" and to the "aim" of the sermon.[23] Concerning black preaching, Henry Mitchell spoke about a "controlling idea" and a "behavioral purpose," which sounds more socially directed than Craddock's notion.[24] Stephen Farris advocated a summary of the biblical text in one sentence that combines Long's focus and function statements.[25]

Jana Childers has revised her own understanding of a theme sentence. For her it used to represent an original insight to the text, but she has dropped that notion because it put an undue burden on her as a preacher and was not meeting the needs of her people. Instead, she opted for something that simply and faithfully connects to the lives of the people. So she wrote, "The purpose of a theme sentence is to help you keep your focus, not to advertise the erudition of your sermon."[26] Alyce M. McKenzie offered a fresh approach (drawing on Wolfgang Iser), speaking of the text as a "theme-horizon" and a theme as a perspective one has on the text, "like the 'You are here' arrow on a map."[27] When she encouraged preachers to preach on wisdom texts, many of which are one-liners, presumably the verse in effect becomes the thesis statement of the sermon around which she clusters experiences.[28]

All of this is to say that the classical notion of a thesis is alive and well in homiletics today, albeit with variations and adaptations. On the need for a theme sentence and an intended result, at least in this group of homileticians, there is a fair degree of consensus.

Double-barreled Variations on a Traditional Theme Sentence

DAVIS	**Using Any Source: An Idea That Grows**	
	What am I to talk about?	What does this mean/ What must be said?
ROBINSON	**Using Any Source: Subject/Complement**	
	What am I talking about?	What am I saying about it?
CRADDOCK	**Using a Biblical/Rhetorical Source**	
	What the text is saying	What the text is doing
LONG	Focus Statement	Function Statement
MITCHELL	Controlling Idea	Behavioral Purpose
WILSON	**Using a Biblical/Theological Source**	
	What is God doing in or behind the text?	What is God doing today?
	The major concern of the text (MCT)	The major concern of the sermon (MCS)
CHAPELL	Fallen Condition Focus (FCF)	How the text addresses the FCF

Assessment of the Theme Sentence Approach

Are all of these various double-barreled options equal? Homileticians have failed to recognize them, much less to discuss and assess them. As we will see, many people continue to write as though the old notion of a theme sentence still prevails. These matters ought to be important for a discipline that aspires to be academic since they represent elemental structures in homiletical composition. Haddon Robinson may be closest to representing the modernist notion of a universal claim in his approach to a theme. Most of the other approaches make more limited particular claims as directed by the biblical text itself. A primary bridge between biblical time and the present is identified using the principle of identity. Bryan Chapell assumes a common identity between people then and now, overlooking historical and cultural differences and rooted in the FCF. Craddock and Long assume an identity between what the text is trying to do and what the sermon is trying to do (i.e., the function statement). I assume an identity between God's action then (MCT) and God's action now (MCS). Sidney Greidanus provides an excellent discussion of both positive and negative ways of bridging the historical-critical gap that go beyond identification.[29] To my mind a focus statement can be important as a way of ensuring that one is reading the text with rhetorical sensitivity, but it does nothing to correct individuals who read the Bible with an anthropocentric rather than revelational focus. In any case, we have at least three different kinds of bridges based in identity (i.e., people then and now, the purpose of the text and the sermon, and God then and God now) and they all may be important, but they need discussion.

More than that, these double-barreled approaches to a theme sentence build into the theme sentence a hermeneutical transition between then and now; they are concerned with both saying and doing what the biblical text says and does, or with what God in the biblical text says and does.

Opposition to a Theme Sentence Approach

A significant number of teachers of homiletics either avoid speaking of a thesis statement or speak against it. David Buttrick, for example, is interested in how sermons form in the consciousness of listeners. Thus he claims, "Homiletic thinking is always *a thinking of theology toward images.*"[30] He is against rationalistic approaches to preaching, such as preaching in three points that develop a single proposition: "Preachers do not explicate teachings; they explore symbols. Faith does have content, but not a content that can be spelled out in propositional statements for instruction."[31]

DAVID BUTTRICK: MOVING INTO FOCUS

Instead, Buttrick advocates a series of "moves," no more than five in a fifteen-minute sermon,[32] each functioning like a camera that brings a "field of meaning" into focus. Each move is to bring the "statement of a move" into "focus"[33] (an anticipation of a "focus statement"?) within the first three sentences–for example, "We are sinners"[34] –and is to conclude with the same idea expressed in a simple sentence: "Compound sentences will not close."[35] Each move is to connect logically with the next one. He seems to reject a thesis statement for the overall sermon, yet he proposes what to all intents and purposes are five thesis statements, one for each "move" and all linked by "connective logic." The end result of this linked chain of ideas, he says, is not an expounding of a truth so much as it is a "bringing into view" through symbols "understandings of God, of God's mysterious purposes, and of unseen wonders of grace in human lives."[36] We may assume that this seeking of God also describes what Buttrick tells students to seek in scripture–as he says, "Preaching is obviously more than talking about the Bible. Preaching...must dare to name God in conjunction with the world of lived experience."[37]

What is the difference between Buttrick's simple-sentence "focus" statements and earlier theme sentences? The difference may not be something that we readily see in analyzing a sermon, for any paragraph is organized around a simple sentence (such as "We are sinners"). The difference also may not be in what we as listeners hear, except in the sense that this sentence will be repeated in some form. The difference may be in the preacher's mind and attitude! Buttrick's statement of the move is not the object of focus in itself; it is the instrument of focus, the lens through which one looks at the Bible and life so that by the end of the viewing, a field of meaning has taken shape in one's mind. This phenomenological way of considering things apparently makes a big difference to the preacher who builds a movement of thought, rather than an argument. For the listeners the statement is just a statement; its function as a lens is not likely to be a matter of conscious awareness. What listeners will notice is whether the paragraph depicts a world coming into focus (though they would not use these terms), as opposed to an intellectual argument. Most homileticians today avoid developing a sermon in strictly linear, abstract, or logical ways. A theme statement approach is based on the value of clear thinking and a certain logical connectedness. Buttrick's stance, from a preacher's perspective, may seem manipulative, not fully respectful, less than forthcoming.

RICHARD L. ESLINGER: A POSTMODERN CULTURAL-LINGUISTIC MODEL

Other homileticians, in following Buttrick, have gone beyond him. Richard L. Eslinger says, "our homilies will not trade in propositions addressed to rationalist minds."[38] Using George Lindbeck and Hans Frei, he argues against earlier hermeneutical models. A cognitive hermeneutic reduced the biblical text to a main idea or a "single point thematic." Meaning was sought in this idea, but the idea itself was external to the text, since the homiletical amplification largely used extra-biblical matter. An experiential-expressive hermeneutic used historical imagination to get behind the text to its origin. This gave that "history" a higher value than the text itself, thereby twisting the text. Preachers then brought subjective stories or illustrations to reinforce the text. In this process, cultural assumptions and ideologies were masked as universal or Christian truths.

Eslinger argues instead for a postliberal cultural-linguistic hermeneutic that interprets scripture within a particular believing community. The best means for that is image and narrative. Eslinger presents a postmodern homiletical alternative to what he conceives as propositional truth in sermons. He argues that,

1. "narratives may be 'meaningful' but never 'true,'" as Frank Kermode says;

2. their truth may be known because the worlds they present are "followable" and have an effective "capacity to overwhelm the hearer";

3. the truth of scripture nonetheless may be evaluated by the "correspondence" of its life with its central story; and,

4. paradigms may represent truth.[39]

His model is Buttrick's linked chain, though without his tight linear thread. Eslinger envisions the sermon as episodic and mobile—either a series of textual images, or a narrative plot, or a mixture of the two. His purpose with scripture is to present its patterns and images with "narrative modesty" (as opposed to the style of propositions), such that the character of God becomes evident through them.[40] Eslinger's approach at times seems reductionist, presenting symbols and imaginative constructs as a stark alternative to abstract reasoning, instead of recognizing the values of both and the limitations of each on its own.

EUGENE L. LOWRY: HOMILETICAL PLOT

Eugene L. Lowry's narrative-based five-stage "homiletical plot" is far from propositional in its structure. For him the sermon will move "primarily by logic movement, or by the shifting impact of image or images, or by the process of a story line."[41] He proposes a variation on the traditional theme sentence that said everything the sermon was going to say. The traditional approach "focused on the *scratch* of the sermon—the final bottom-line conclusion. Contrariwise, what I am suggesting is to name the central *itch*."[42] This "itch" will be an issue, not a resolution, and will address: "What is at stake here, the presenting difficulty that will take a sermon to work through?"[43] He wants the sermon to be tentative, evocative, poetic, and "dancing the edge of mystery" (a phrase from Buttrick that Lowry honors by his use of it for his book's title). He looks in a text for something that will "draw people beyond the message that is being articulated into the presence of God."[44] More specifically, he wants something bothersome that will lead to the aim of the sermon, which is "to *evoke* the proclamation."[45]

LUCY ROSE AND JOHN MCCLURE: COLLABORATIVE, ROUNDTABLE MODELS

Lucy Rose and John McClure have gone farther than others in rejecting any notion of a central thesis. They have devised "collaborative" and "roundtable" approaches to preaching. Both see the sermon as an open process with no closure. McClure advocates meeting with a group of people and allowing the conversation to generate the sermon. The sermon will proceed as a series of sequences, akin to Buttrick's moves, but each composed of four codes or perspectives: theo-symbolic (worldview), semantic (truth/meaning), cultural (experience), and scriptural (anamnesis/memory).[46] Both McClure and Rose reject what they see as the preacher's traditional hierarchical authority in favor of the authority of the community. Thus in their view the sermon is a communal venture, and the preacher has no special corner on meaning. Meaning arises out of community and experience. The preacher's task is to uphold and reflect the community's views. Because the sermon is open-ended, individuals will draw their own meanings from what is said.

Rose dismisses the possibility of articulating truth because she believes that language is always bias-laden. For her, the sermon itself is a search for meaning; it explores various interpretations and makes proposals and wagers.[47] It is multi-focused[48] and tentative.[49] In this extreme kind of postmodern alternative, a single theme sentence has no place. It fosters authoritarian notions of communication and practices of preaching. It implies an understanding that language makes direct and certain reference to the reality to which it points. It invokes outdated notions of revelation. For Rose, a preacher treats scripture not so much as a source of revelation but as "the record of the experiences of our foremothers and forefathers who wrestled with God and what it meant to live as God's people."[50] Out of the community's own conversations one listens for the divine.

Homiletical Analysis

We have focused on one of the most basic elements in homiletics, how the biblical meanings connect with the sermon. We have observed different ports of call for the sermon's thesis statement, and we have seen a broad spectrum of responses in various harbors up and down the homiletical coast. Reu, like John Albert Broadus before him, regarded the thesis statement as a welcome and objective expression of the unity of the text—the text could be captured effectively in a propositional statement.

The Course Options

Farther down the coast a thesis statement discovers no easy passage. Buttrick substitutes five mini-theses for the thesis statement. These effectively add up to the charted course of the sermon. Lowry's "central itch" or issue of the sermon does not accommodate a thesis statement and does not provide any resolution, while somehow pointing beyond itself to something greater. Eslinger, McClure, and Rose toss the theme sentence overboard like an unwanted anchor and chain, for it holds their conversational sermons back from what is needed in these new times.

Another group argues for the importance of a thesis statement, albeit with a much modified and double-barreled approach. We have then two different kinds of consensus. If our discussion were simply about one sentence, we would have spent far too long on it already, but it is about much more than that. It has to do with sermon form and substance that reveal fundamental assumptions about preaching and about preaching the Bible. Ought teachers of preaching simply say to their students, "These two approaches represent an impasse and you choose for yourself"?

The Course Difficulty

The intersection of the Bible and the sermon is difficult for at least three reasons:

1. Some homileticians are imprecise or vague on the issue of biblical meanings, although it seems basic to preaching.

2. What homileticians look for in biblical texts is often part of an entire system of homiletical procedure. One cannot just look on the shelf for the jar marked "Biblical Meanings," pull it out, and expect biblical meaning to come out on its own. It is a sticky jar, and other jars are bound to come with it. These have labels as diverse as: philosophy of language, authority of scripture, the preacher's role, the function of experience, the role of the congregation, sermon form, the goal of preaching, and others.

3. Homiletics is not as pastoral or academic a discipline as it needs to be. By pastoral I mean—among other things—practical. Homileticians at times are too interested in devising new paradigms and not interested enough in how effective or helpful they are, or how faithful they are to the call to preach the gospel of Christ. By academic I mean critically responsible for what has been written in homiletical literature. Publishers

may contribute to the problem, for they are not always concerned with whether an author is in conversation with the field. Further, homiletics is necessarily interdisciplinary. Homileticians try to import categories to homiletics without doing careful spadework to determine how those categories might translate into sermons. Of course, even notions of what is effective and practical are value laden and open to interpretation. One cannot expect to find uniformity of opinion. Still, given the nature of homiletics, a minimal standard can be: Can a typical preacher readily understand a proposed method and implement it effectively? Is its effectiveness demonstrated in actual sermons? Does it represent a faithful proclamation of the gospel?

The Listener and the Thesis Statement

In my own thinking we are not at an impasse on the question of thesis statement, at least from the perspective of how listeners hear sermons. With any sermon, listeners venture a guess as to what they think the preacher said for the simple reason that rational thought has structure that listeners seek even when it is absent. A congregation ought to be able to describe their understanding of a sermon in one sentence. Two central standards for sermon excellence can be:

1. Listeners find meaning.
2. The meaning corresponds to the gospel message.

In most meaningful communication, sentences link to sentences, paragraphs link to paragraphs, and sections link to sections until a whole is produced in which the parts and whole contribute to each other. In homiletics, the issue is not only whether these links are present in the sermon but also how they are used to direct composition and to influence the congregation.

Homileticians who reject a thesis statement most often reject a classical model of thesis statement, such as Reu employed, without noting the many newer models that have been developed. Their practice may be a good rhetorical strategy because, if nothing else, it helps to make an important point. In Puritan plain style preaching and its present day derivations, preachers commonly study a biblical text until it yields a doctrine. Once the thesis is framed the biblical text is ignored while the preacher romps through various proof texts that display similar doctrines. The thesis sentence in such cases seems external to the text itself and points outside it, though not always outside of the Bible. The thesis is often presented as if it is an objective statement of self-evident truth, the essential kernel of textual truth to which a congregation should give its intellectual assent. Historically, it has tended to be seen as a male model because of its emphasis on logic. Authority seemed to rest in the preacher, while the congregation merely received. The text itself (from our own contemporary perspective) was discarded as a winnowed husk.

Such preaching may still be found, but none of the homileticians we have named since Reu embrace it. Already by 1958, Davis had insisted that the theme not be confined to propositional abstraction but that it include "realities of the human heart." The thesis sentence cannot be an objective statement of truth. Rather it is commonly an interpretation of a text–not the only one, not even necessarily the best one, and certainly not a complete one. It is simply the best pointer the preacher can discern under the limitations of the pastor's week.

Many of these homileticians would agree with Davis's idea of the sermon as something organic that grows. None would place sole emphasis on words and ideas, and all would affirm that scripture itself has themes, images, symbols, and narratives, not just arguments. When Buttrick conceives of several linked moves that can each be stated in a sentence, on one level he is simply opting for essential clarity.[51] Buttrick's own purpose may be to use symbols to shape consciousness. His intention may assist its accomplishment; but when theory is translated into practice, a sentence is still a sentence, and listeners can still legitimately venture a thesis statement for a sermon as a whole by asking, "What is he/she talking about?"

When I select a particular concern of the text (as opposed to the MCT) for development into one or more paragraphs in the sermon, I do something that is not far removed from Buttrick's idea of a statement of a move. An individual aspect of a text–be it an idea, an event in the plot, or the significance of an image[52]–becomes an organizing principle. It may be developed in the sermon in linear, reasoned ways, or it may be like the bud of a flower, around which thoughts and images will cluster and unfurl as petals. However, what I designate as the MCT is one sentence among several possibilities that focuses on a gracious action of God in the biblical text and becomes the theme sentence of the sermon. God is the focus. God's action is empowering. Moreover, the theme sentence is double-barreled since it has its partner statement, the major concern of the sermon, which ensures that the preacher will stay focused in moving from the text to today.

Critics who do away with theme sentences do not recognize the changes that have taken place. It would be a mistake to think of the major concern of the text as *the idea* of the text, as though it is a tea bag that merely awaits hot water to release the full flavor of the text. It would be a further mistake to think of it as an "objective" dogmatic claim addressed solely to the mind; it points to God's action. Instead of asserting, "This is so and must be accepted," it invites participation, "Come and see what God is doing." Those who dismiss theme sentences make a further mistake; a theme sentence in itself does not have the autocratic authority they seem to ascribe to it. A preacher might choose to use a theme sentence in authoritarian ways, but one ought not confuse the instrument with how it is handled. In short, the problem of paternalistic preaching is not best addressed by deletion of a thesis sentence. A well-deployed thesis sentence can be a listener's best friend.

The Authority of the Text

It is one thing to acknowledge that interpretation of a biblical text is necessarily tentative and dependent upon biases and points of view. It is another thing so to value abnegation of authority that the tentative becomes the goal. Then no authority claim is made, and no one really knows what the preacher is getting at. This can be the result in sermons that offer no closure. Listeners cannot determine the sermon's significance. Paul commands Christ's followers to "be transformed by the renewing of your minds, so that you may discern what is the will of God" (Rom. 12:2). The sermon should invite Christians to think in significant ways about significant matters of faith and life. Avoiding a thesis statement can be a form of tyranny, for the preacher demands that the listeners discover the preacher's meaning without offering what is needed. Once the congregation knows with confidence what is being said, they have genuine freedom to react. Preachers who use thesis statements often do so out of respect for their congregations as listeners. They may also use such statements to form consciousness or to invite participation in a metaphor or story, as opposed to presenting something objective for consciousness merely to receive. Preachers use thesis statements to witness to God as clearly as possible in order to equip the saints for ministry.

In this chapter we have been doing more than looking at theme sentences. We have been asking, What does a preacher look for in a biblical text? To preach the Bible does not ensure that the gospel is preached, thus the preacher needs to look for the word of God, assessing the text as revelation. We have seen the classical model of theme sentence in Reu that had no requirements beyond being a complete declarative sentence. We have also seen a new double-barreled understanding of thesis statement, for example in Davis, Robinson (subject, complement, big idea), Craddock, Long (focus statement, function statement), Wilson (MCT/MCS) and Chapell (FCF and theme). Each has its own advantages, yet the latter ones are the only ones that seem directly to require focus on God; Wilson alone puts the further requirement of a short sentence with God as the subject and grace as its theological thrust. More than that, these double-barreled approaches build into the theme sentence a link between then and now; they are concerned with both saying and doing, whether this emphasis is on what the biblical text says and does, or on what God in the biblical text says and does.

These issues are important, for the theme sentence is the sermon in microcosm, and something inept or out of place at this level will affect the entire sermon. By the same token, a sermon that does not have a theme sentence is likely to remain out of focus during its composition and delivery. For sermons to move in nonauthoritarian ways, homiletical discussions need to move beyond outdated assessments of classical themes to new designations that get at the heart of the sermon and how the sermon moves from the text to today.

2

EXEGESIS FOR PREACHING

Homileticians spend considerable time talking about exegesis. Classes in Bible deal with exegesis and biblical interpretation. Is it, then, really necessary for homileticians to cover the same ground? Given that biblical scholars may outnumber homileticians by roughly seventeen-to-one, is this the best use of scarce homiletical resources? Should not teachers of preaching spend most of their time on sermon form and substance, composition and delivery?[1] In their publications, homileticians seem to devote more time to pre-sermon activities with the Bible than to the sermon itself. Is this appropriate? We will see that homiletics does need to concern itself with exegetical matters, for with many current methods of reading texts—for example, reader response—the text seems less fixed. It can become anything someone chooses to make of it. Biblical texts are much more fluid than they have been, and the interpretative enterprise itself has become more fluid and more playful.

Learning Biblical Exegesis

The book that most instructed me in how to do biblical exegesis is a slim volume by two internationally known biblical scholars, Otto Kaiser and Werner G. Kümmel, *Exegetical Method: A Student's Handbook.*[2] Their way of talking about exegesis would not be accepted today: Exegesis for them was a "scientific" process that asks two kinds of questions, one concerning the historical origin of the text and the situation of its hearers and the other concerning "the objective meaning of the text."[3] Any interpretation violates the text if it fails "to bring the historical meaning of the text, in its historical context, to light."[4]

The Exegetical Steps

The steps Kümmel outlines for introductory New Testament exegesis perhaps are familiar to most preachers, yet they are nonetheless instructive to review:

1. Use a reliable edition of the Greek New Testament, paying attention to its critical apparatus to see if there are textual problems or variant readings of the selected text.

2. Outline the sequence of thoughts in the specific text with a view to its structure.

3. Identify key words and phrases that might be thematic clues; check in a concordance or lexicon for meanings of important words.

4. Make a provisional translation of the original language.

5. Using specialized commentaries, determine the text's boundaries: What is its immediate context, and to what larger section does it belong?

6. Read in a comprehensive commentary about the historical context and prehistory of the biblical text, exploring for instance its original form and use; if it has been changed, discover why.

7. Determine what the author means to say in the larger work.

8. Check to see if the text has parallels elsewhere or cites other texts that might give clues about the source.

9. Seek the meaning of a text "in its oldest attestable form" (44) and in the form, for instance, that an evangelist or Jesus used it.

10. Venture an interpretation of the text.[5]

The Changing Face of Exegesis

During the years since Kaiser and Kümmel wrote in the 1960s, the means of historical textual investigation has remained largely intact, but attitudes and practices have changed dramatically. Scholars seem to agree that interpretation is inescapably bias-laden because interpreters, like their texts, are found in historical settings. All texts have what Ricoeur called a "surplus of meaning": They have many meanings, not just one. We now speak of a range of meanings or of an arena of interpretation. Even to determine what are authentic or legitimate meanings depends upon points of view, for no one point of view can be claimed as "right"; thus most interpretations are necessarily tentative. Such a climate can easily become relativistic; texts themselves become fluid for they can become anything an interpreter wants to make of them. The authority of scripture (however we might understand it) to govern the faith and doctrine of the church can be seriously eroded.

Relativism is not the only alternative in this fluid situation. Theological statements can still be evaluated and tested. The process simply needs to be identified within the specific cultural settings of the interpreter. The act of biblical interpretation, once considered a "science," has joined the arts as a process, for as Richard B. Hays says, "Because exegesis is an art rather than a science, no single mechanical procedure can be prescribed."[6]

Exegetical Literature

Not many books on basic biblical exegesis *per se* have appeared in the decades since 1967.[7] This relative scarcity is surprising given the importance of the subject, not least for theology, history, archeology, and homiletics. Discussion of exegesis is not limited to Bible studies. Theory and practice of exegesis accounted for nearly one sixth of M. Reu's thorough *Homiletics* in 1922,[8] and in the house of homiletics the subject has never been further away than the back porch. Recently it has found its way back into the kitchen, prompted in part by Leander E. Keck, who propped open the screen door. His classic *The Bible in the Pulpit*[9] sounded a call for the renewal of preaching based on the Bible. He called for preachers to engage the concrete issues to which biblical texts were addressed and to recognize "that what biblical writers found necessary to say was determined not by truth in general but by needs in particular."[10] The task for preachers was not to expound some broad truth but to focus on "the way one correlates the original readers and today's readers."[11]

Several homileticians, starting in the early 1980s, heeded his call to give the Bible more attention in preaching,[12] yet a few need special mention. A key book was Donald M. Wardlaw's *Preaching Biblically: Creating Sermons in the Shape of Scripture*,[13] a project of the Academy of Homiletics that changed the way many homileticians viewed biblical preaching: It was a novel idea that biblical forms might have implications for sermon form, not just content. In 1984 Ronald J. Allen published his *Contemporary Biblical Interpretation for Preaching*,[14] which spread before preachers a whole range of new critical ways they might read biblical texts beyond historical criticism–for example, form; redaction; structuralism; and sociological, liberation, and canonical criticism.[15] In 1989 Thomas G. Long published his influential *Preaching and the Literary Forms of the Bible,* exposing preachers to rhetorically sensitive ways of reading texts.[16] He was concerned with how the biblical text guides the reading process by creating in the reader certain rhetorical effects. He set a new agenda for the preacher: "He or she must not attempt to say and do everything the text once said and did. Rather the preacher should attempt to say and do what a *portion* of the text *now* says and does for a new and unique set of people."[17]

More recently David L. Bartlett published his *Between the Bible and the Church: New Methods for Biblical Preaching,* a book that provides a conservative defense of historical criticism, yet is more radical than it may appear.[18] His model for the preacher is the scribe in Matthew 13:52 who is trained for the kingdom of heaven and brings forth something old and new.[19] He wants preachers to be concerned with the world in which the text was created (something old) but he wants preachers to be more concerned with the narrative world the biblical text creates. He looks to new movements in criticism that give the preacher access to the world in front of the text, behind the text, and the world we bring to the text.[20] He says of his student who preached on the prodigal son's mother that, "She certainly stretched the text beyond its usual boundaries, but it was *that* text she stretched."[21] Above all he wants preachers to be creative and free in making links not only with life today but also with other biblical texts that seem to echo one's primary text, whether the Bible writer intended these echoes or not.[22] My own, *God Sense: Reading the Bible for Preaching,* looks in another direction for creativity in biblical interpretation. The ancient and medieval preachers had four senses or lenses with which they viewed any text to discover their sermons: literal, moral, eschatological, and christological. Preachers can learn from the preaching tradition of the church how to do better in the art of theological interpretation of scripture.[23]

The Reappearance of Exegesis

It may be significant that after a long hiatus, exegesis once again is a subject in textbooks in homiletics, for instance by Fred Craddock, Tom Long, Stephen Farris, Ron Allen, and myself.[24] (For some reason this is not the case in key homiletics books that are firmly in the evangelical camp–perhaps because the authority of scripture is less tested there.[25]) Many factors may contribute to the homiletical reappearance of exegesis:

1. Biblical studies itself is undergoing transition; hermeneutical theorists like Paul Ricoeur and Eric D. Hirsch have revolutionized interpretation theory, for instance, with contrasting views on whether we can get back to the original author through the text and on the multi-valency of texts.

2. Incoming students to seminary have less experience with the Bible and need additional help rendering it for the church.

3. The biblical studies field is going in directions that do not easily speak of the Bible as the word of God, and thus it does not help preaching as much as it might. Biblical scholars cannot always be trusted to look at what is important for preaching, namely, the Bible as scripture and revelation.

4. Homileticians have developed an increased awareness that historical criticism, essential as it is, is no longer adequate preparation for the pulpit in itself. Biblical theology has long been aware of this and has sought ways to bring biblical texts into conversation with tradition and contemporary issues.[26]

5. The exegetical method many homileticians were taught needs to be expanded to take account of new understandings and methods in interpretation.

New Exegetical Guidelines and Preaching

How are some of the new homiletical guidelines for exegesis different from what went before? First, they are geared for preachers. Some of the earlier models seem more suited for preparing to write a learned commentary than for a busy pastor trying to treat scripture responsibly for Sunday. Fred Craddock presents a compressed process that starts with *reading the text aloud,* a playful exercise that allows time for reflection, note taking, questioning, and naïve enjoyment. This reading ensures three things: familiarity with the text; identification with listeners "who will come to the text unaided except for their own thoughts, feelings, and needs"; and discovery of material for the introduction of the sermon itself.[27] The preacher then can *establish the text* by checking for variant readings in the notes of a study Bible. (This is not the same thing as checking different translations.) The next step is to *determine the parameters of the text* to ensure that the unit is complete and to identify smaller units within it. Craddock then advocates *placing the biblical text within its historical, literary, and theological settings.*[28]

Because exegesis is no longer seen as an objective science, attention is now given to the role of the interpreter in the process. This is reflected not least in Craddock's final two steps. The interpreter is to *become aware of "one's point of contact with the text."*[29] This has to do with (a) the level at which one engages the text (does one preach on Jesus' words, or on the tradition of interpretation Matthew has received about those words, or on his interpretation of that tradition?) and, (b) the reader's point of identity within the text (a relationship that Craddock says is needed "to distance oneself from the text and to begin thinking of oneself as the person who will share with the church what the text says"[30]). Finally, the preacher is to *put the text "into one's own words"* by stating what one has heard and experienced in it, namely the answers to the questions, "What is the text saying?" and "What is the text doing?"(his double-barreled theme sentence).[31] Anyone wanting to know how to do this in a fresh way might turn, as we have said, to Eugene Peterson's *The Message.*

Exegesis may also have become more playful, not as a way of trivializing the activity, but of honoring its complexity and the need for preachers to be open to new perspectives. The interpreter's curiosity is key: David Bartlett says, "it is no sin to use imagination to discover or suggest ways in which one text may play with or play off another. Scripture itself plays such word games all the time."[32] Tom Long sees a process of questioning the text to be "a creative, imaginative activity, something like brainstorming."[33] Before preachers go to any secondary sources or explore the text historically, Long encourages them to ask questions on everything. They need to inquire about details that might seem out of place in the text. They should also ask how the text would look from the perspective of a range of people–young and old, rich and poor, male and female, churched and unchurched, and people of other races.[34] I have suggested that students read the text and then use imagination to retell its story (whatever its actual form) to others as a means to discover what it says.[35]

Exegetical Creativity

Other volumes are not about exegesis per se, but they give glimpses of the creativity needed for the exegetical process. Ever since Charles L. Rice published *Imagination and Interpretation* (1970),[36] the subject of imagination has been important for homiletics, as seen in numerous works.[37] Two recent books edited by Jana Childers and

Cleophus J. LaRue ask women and African American preachers, respectively, to discuss the creative process they follow. The results are often fascinating.[38] One woman's sermon began at length with information about breeding dogs. It then moved into faith and denominational purity. Toward the end this preacher noted, "It is interesting to me that Jesus called the Syrophoenician woman a dog." She called for the church not to try to purify itself by inbreeding, but by going beyond itself and relying upon the Holy Spirit.[39]

Numerous other edited volumes contain complete sermons coupled with reviews of current homiletical theory.[40]

Interactive Exegesis

Earlier models for exegesis assumed that the reader was like a miner looking for a gold vein. Now the process is discussed in more relational and interactive terms.[41] The identity of the text, the reader, and the congregation are respected. The reader is an active participant, for example, in Stephen Farris's ten-step model of exegesis, which he recommends following before going to any commentaries.[42] His questions deal insightfully with many of the issues we have already named in relation to Kaiser, Kümmel, and Craddock concerning historical and literary matters, including these innovative questions. (1) "What is the movement of my passage?"–this question recognizes that structure of a text should no longer be thought of as static and may be sketched "using block, line and circles, or other devices, and label the parts."[43] (2) "What is unusual, striking, perhaps even offensive to contemporary ears about this passage?"[44] Farris says that the "enemy of good preaching is not opposition or even emotional revulsion to the text; it is disinterest. Identifying the negative reaction and making use of it is an effective way of defeating disinterest."[45] Perhaps most intriguing is his suggestion that the ten steps be repeated: Do them once before any commentaries are consulted and once after.[46] He also provides two helpful lists of questions. The first list comprises a prior exegesis of the situation, asking the age of the listeners, their educational background, their expectations of the minister and of the sermon, and what they will have difficulty hearing from the preacher.[47] The second list comprises a prior exegesis of the self, asking, for example, what are the life circumstances of people I have most difficulty relating to, what "issues or pastoral situations might I be tempted to avoid," and in what ways will my personality be a help and hindrance in my ministry?[48]

Something important happens here. The situation and setting of preaching is not left in the deep freeze to the end of the process, as in the old models. The interpreter is acknowledged to be present from the beginning, subtly influencing the choices that are made. I encourage preachers to venture an appropriate focus on what God is doing in or behind the biblical text early in the preparation process so that the exegetical process will then test and sharpen that focus.

Exegesis in both biblical studies and homiletics has become literary as well as historical. Literary criticism teaches people to come to texts with different lenses that allow them to see different things: Formalist criticism emphasizes those dimensions of a text that give it unity; feminist criticism studies attitudes toward women; and new historicism considers the historical and economic contexts of culture. There are many other kinds of literary criticism (e.g., reader response, Marxist, rhetorical, structuralist, deconstruction, postcolonial). Each one offers different lenses allowing one to see things in the text one might not otherwise see. Each offers its own interpretations. This is one reason we speak of texts having a "surplus of meaning," and of literary criticism as being so important for biblical studies and preaching.

Exegesis must become more theological as well; Leander Keck's call for the recovery of the Bible in the pulpit is perhaps not adequate in itself for our time. Preachers may have good theology, but they need help and permission to read texts theologically, as the church has always done when reading the Bible as scripture, as revelation. In *God Sense,* I provide thirty theological questions for preachers to bring to the text, beyond the historical and literary. These include: What group or person represents God in this text? What does this text say about who God is? What human brokenness or vulnerability does this text reveal? What divine judgment rests upon those in this text who inflict brokenness or who take advantage of the vulnerable? What hope does this text imply? What does God do in this text to provide or accomplish what is needed? What other central biblical texts display similar actions of God? What does this text say, imply, anticipate, or echo about Jesus Christ? What does the fact of the resurrection say to this text?[49] Such questions help to keep the agenda of the preacher where it needs to be, and they allow the preacher to benefit fully from some of the new ways of reading the Bible without losing sight of its purpose for preaching. However, homiletics as a whole is not yet at this place, and in order for it to become so, it will need to undergo a paradigm shift to put God at the center of scripture. Until that time, the Bible may be in the pulpit and God may still be absent.

Exegesis, Hermeneutics, and Homiletics

The Basic Vocabulary

One of the most important shifts in recent times concerns three terms: exegesis, hermeneutics, and homiletics. The distinction between these terms has never been absolute, and root meanings help us to see the problem. The Greek *exegeomai* means to explain or interpret. Thus exegesis is an explanation or interpretation of a text. It tends to connote an historical approach that determines what the text said and meant for its first hearers.

Hermes is the Greek messenger god. Hermeneutics is thus the study of how messages mean something to the recipient. This also implies an explanation or interpretation. Hermeneutics tends to connote a two-way process of bringing the text's meaning forward to today across cultural and other barriers and of bringing worldly reality to bear fully on the text.

Homiletics is from *homileo*, Greek for "to crowd together" (as in a conversation or as the congregations did to hear a sermon in the pew-less ancient settings). *Homilia* is a company or association of people and then the conversation they carry on, while *homilos* is the crowd or throng. Thus in its root meaning a homily is a conversation with a crowd, while homiletics is the art of developing and delivering that conversation. Homiletics in the past has tended to connote taking the meaning of the text and applying it to the specific life and work of a congregation.

To a degree, all three of these terms crowd together in preaching, the boundaries between them becoming blurred. These three terms and the actions they represent were traditionally understood to be like three consecutive buses a preacher took between the Bible and the sermon in what we might imagine to be Sermon City. Early in the week preachers used to board the Exegesis bus and travel up Bible Boulevard through the historical district of town where they would engage historical critical exegesis. They would then transfer to the Hermeneutics bus for the trip up the newer end of town to Today Street, during which they came to understand the significance of the text for today. At this point, biblical interpretation was effectively finished, and the direction for the sermon was clear. Preachers got off the Hermeneutics bus and transferred to the Homiletics bus for the rest of the journey up to the church, during which they applied their understandings to the particularities of the congregation's life and work.

Recent Shifts in Understanding

Several things have changed in recent decades:

1. Exegesis is less distinctly a scientific method and often becomes a hermeneutical process that varies from text to text. In earlier decades access to the text was primarily diachronic (historical through time)—in other words centered exclusively in historical criticism. Now it is also synchronic (contemporary, at the same time). Literary criticism allows for direct and immediate appreciation of the text through such things as narrative plot, character, emotion, and other kinds of analysis.

2. Textual interpretation was formerly thought to stop once the meaning for today was secured. The scholarly task of biblical study was complete, and the baton was handed over to the preacher to carry the sermon to the finish line. There has been a shift, however. Now, interpretation of the text is not so easily confined. It continues throughout sermon composition as a preacher represents the text within the sermon and even in the pulpit where further adjustments are made during delivery. In other words, as preachers we have no interpretation of the text until we have said what we have to say about it in the sermon. The interpretation of the text is the sermon, not something else that we have received along the way from various sources.

3. Before, preachers were not to engage a text in personal ways until its singular meaning had been determined. Now preachers are to engage the text in both scholarly and personal ways as a means to determine its multiple meanings. To some extent preachers cannot help but do so.

4. Preachers used to be encouraged to spend most of the week studying the biblical text and reading widely. They were to turn to composition only late in the week. I left seminary with the impression (intended by my professors or not, mistaken as I was or not) that good biblical exegesis and wide reading took me 80 percent of the way into the pulpit. Some scholars seem to reinforce such thinking, "If the sermon is pervasively biblical, the preacher's task is preeminently exegetical."[50] I tried to arrange my week that way. I spent most of my total preparation time doing critical study, without even beginning composition. In so doing I learned that a preacher is relatively

safe in dealing with what the text meant; but when one turns to its significance today, the ride becomes bumpy, preachers have to take risks, and many seek to delay the experience. Walter Brueggemann, even in writing a commentary designed for preachers, expresses some of this dis-ease:

> The farther one moves away from "then" toward "now," the more the risks increase. On the one hand, that is because we have no methodological consensus about how to move from "then" to "now," or even if it is legitimate to make the move. On the other hand, the move very much depends on the interpreter's judgment about the needs and prospects of the present situation, a judgment inevitably personal.[51]

I am no less committed to the importance of careful exegesis than I once was. I do think the total percentage of time a preacher (at least experienced preachers) can devote primarily to the historical analysis of the text is much lower, perhaps around 30 percent of the total time for sermon preparation. Literary, theological, and congregational interpretation require much of the time in sermon composition. My suggestion is to begin composition early in the week (Monday or Tuesday) and spread through to the end (Friday), being disciplined in one's use of time and taking advantage of as much time as possible for gestation.[52]

The Homiletical Task

Just as biblical interpretation now extends from the beginning to the end of the sermon process, so too is the case with homiletics. Originally reserved for the end of the process, it now moves closer to the beginning. Preachers start thinking about the congregations to which they will preach from the moment of their earliest reading of the text. This occurs, for instance, in Craddock's first step of reading the text aloud. In his *Preaching,* he devotes chapter 5 to interpreting the listeners, chapter 6 to interpreting the text, and chapter 7 to their interconnection. Further, much is lost in the old way of devoting most of the week to reading and note taking, and then only at the end of the week starting to draw one's notes together. Working from notes can be like trying to make a pot of tea from a used tea bag. What was once hot is now cold, and even warming it up will only produce tinted water. In the common course of things a preacher gains energy from working a text and other sources. The same energy that prompts note taking can be channeled just as easily into early paragraphs of a sermon draft.

A suitable model for today is not a preacher taking three successive buses–exegesis, hermeneutics, homiletics. Nor is it the image of a biblical scholar handing a baton to a preacher at the end of the interpretative phase of a relay race. Rather, we might conceive of a single bus filled with folks huddled in conversation in three groupings.

The first group is having a conversation about exegesis. Another group including Bible commentators, theologians, and preachers is talking about hermeneutics. A third group is talking about homiletics, including people from the congregation and from the preacher's own circle of family and acquaintances. These conversations happen simultaneously on the one bus. The circles of conversation are not clearly divided. Sometimes people in one group turn to join another. The preacher fluidly moves back and forth from conversation to conversation as the bus makes its way along Bible Boulevard and Today Street up to the church. The weekly route may be the same, but each journey is different, for different people are on board according to the specific text and contemporary events in focus. In this model, homiletics shifts from being third-in-a-sequence to being one element of a threefold parallel activity of exegesis, hermeneutics, and homiletics.

The Fluid Text

In the above shift, one 1983 volume was pivotal–Don Wardlaw's *Preaching Biblically: Creating Sermons in the Shape of Scripture.*[53] Edmund Steimle, Fred Craddock, Charles Rice, and others had already laid the foundation for allowing scripture to influence the sermon's shape as they worked on preaching narrative texts in narrative ways.[54] However, when Wardlaw's group of homileticians from the Academy of Homiletics arrived on the block and began building, the neighbors took notice. This house had a new form; they were working off of new plans. Sermons apparently could be shaped: by the language of the text (Ronald Allen); by the human and stylistic context of the text (Don Wardlaw); by plotting the text's claim on us (Thomas Long); by the interplay of text and metaphor (Rice); by the structure of the text (William J. Carl III); by the shape of text and preacher (Gardner Taylor); and by the encounter of text with preacher (Thomas Troeger). In the words of a review in *The Christian Century,* "What is new in this case is the notion that preaching ought to be 'biblical' not only in the theological content but also in form and style."[55] In other words, these preachers recognized that preaching is no tail on the exegetical dog; they could discern the creativity of the sermon from the text itself. They experienced themselves to be most creative when they could feel the text move between the past and the present. Homiletics is no mere receptacle for the learning of others; it is an interpretative field in its own right with its own rhetorical goals, objectives, and strategies for accomplishing them.

The Effects of Texts

The notion that texts shape sermons needed further development for it to reach its full potential for preaching. Thomas Long looked beyond the obvious formal differences among biblical texts and discovered different effects these forms had on their hearers. He realized that these effects were part of the meaning of the texts. Rhetorical criticism said as much, but Long took one important additional step that was like the first footprint on the moon. He said that the hermeneutical significance of a biblical text's literary form "should exert influence in the production of a sermon."[56] He did not say that sermons should imitate the form of the text—a sermon on a letter should be a letter, for instance. Rather, he said that, "The preacher should attempt to say and do what a *portion* of the text *now* says and does for a new and unique set of people."[57] A psalm might "[swivel] the universe on the hinges of a single image."[58] The preacher should be attentive to the effect of the image on the imagination and seek to create a similar effect in the sermon. Or a sermon on 1 Corinthians 12:31–14:1 could follow Paul's rhetorical challenges to quarrelling groups and end with a vision of unity and moving forward.[59] Long explored proverbs, narratives, and parables. Mike Graves followed his lead and took a clutch of additional New Testament forms and discussed them in relation to excellent sermons.[60] Most recently, Bruce E. Shields studied the oral features of New Testament texts and argued that the task of preachers is to actualize the gospel (a notion borrowed from Gerhard von Rad), not conceptualize it. The term is a good one though he may have posed these too starkly as alternatives. Preachers can actualize texts not by merely imitating the forms of the early church but by using their own approach. They may do this by "presenting the good news of Jesus Christ in words and forms familiar enough to our hearers that they will hear and permit God to work on every aspect of their lives."[61]

A New Vision of the Text

All of this implies a rhetorical and performative dimension of texts, a greater degree of interaction with them on the part of readers, and ultimately a different vision of the biblical text itself in the homiletical process. When historical critical exegesis was a good preacher's almost exclusive doorway to a biblical text, the text was treated as if it were a fragment of pottery unearthed in an archeological dig. One did not just pick it up. One treated it as an object of historical respect, a repository of knowledge, both in itself and its location. It needed to be photographed in the dirt. The level at which it was found needed to be clearly measured and mapped. Then it needed to be removed and examined, using responsible laboratory techniques. For all that a text might tell us, it was nonetheless an object, an inert thing, something that passively received the scientific things we did to it and eventually yielded its objective meaning.

That image is no longer adequate because, as we have seen, our methods have expanded to include literary and other approaches. Our science is more appropriately now considered an art, since we admit that all our readings include some measure of subjectivity and that we now contend with many legitimate meanings. Biblical theologians now find support for their method of expanding biblical texts so that they are in conversation with other texts and with theology and the church. In other words, opening a text it is like dipping into a pool of meanings. The text, far from being an object that is inert, fixed, and constant, is more like a fluid substance. Its homiletical boundaries are harder to determine. A biblical scholar may define a text as a unit of scripture. But in homiletics is the text of a sermon more appropriately considered to be that unit *along with* its intertextual connections to the entire gospel message? The primary purpose of preaching is not to preach the pericope (a relatively fixed thing) but to preach the gospel (a much more fluid notion that is typically represented in the creeds of the church). The particular text is simply the essential instrument that opens the word of God for today. In any case, the text is rarely just the text. It is the text plus whatever meanings traditionally have been attached to it. This means that to read the text as though its historical critical and theological backgrounds are not part of it is often doing an injustice to the text.

Changing Text under Changing Perspectives

The text is always changing, depending upon the angle from which we look at it. Moreover, each time we read it, we affect how it appears, for we come from a new situation with an altered perspective. The text changes much like a pool does when you put your hand into it. Now we appreciate the tremendous fluid energy within the text that is waiting to be released. The energy flows among it, other biblical texts, and ourselves.

When we deal with a text, we are affected by it. In fact, we cannot properly understand the text until we have entered into it, immersed ourselves in its water, and experienced what it has to say. This is not primarily an historical exercise to find out what it might have felt like back then. It is an essential interpretative activity without which the text can have no significant present meaning. Though different interpretative activities are still implied, the boundaries between them all are increasingly blurred, for the text is fluid. The end product is less an individual act of interpretation that will stand for some time. It is rather understood to be a moment in a process that has passing definition and relevance. It is like thrown water when the splash is caught mid-air in a photograph.

In this chapter we have been dealing with how the Bible is handled for preaching. We have been outlining what has changed in recent decades concerning how preachers approach the biblical text. What was for Kaiser and Kümmel a scientific and objective process dealing with a fixed and static text has become a relational enterprise in which the situation and character of the preacher and the congregation are recognized from the beginning to have an important role. The text itself is always changing, depending upon one's perspective, thus it has a more fluid character, and its boundaries for preaching tend to be less fixed as one hears from other biblical texts echoes of one's own. The act of reading the Bible for preaching has also become more playful and creative. God still needs to be recovered at the center of scripture, and the objective of preaching still needs to shift from preaching a pericope to preaching the gospel of Jesus Christ.

3

HOMILETICIANS
AND THE BIBLE

This chapter seeks to provide an overview of how homileticians have engaged the Bible to assist preaching. The Bible has authority for the church because it continues to be understood as the word of God for the community of faith. Commentaries on the Bible have been written since the early church and preachers usually wrote them. Despite many problems with scholarly commentaries in modern times,[1] we can point to a recent positive sign–the appearance of several series of biblical commentaries written with preachers and preaching in mind. We will examine them to ask in what ways they help preachers, and in particular, how they are of assistance in helping preachers to find and speak of God in the texts. Do they help preachers to reclaim the Bible as scripture? Many of these books offer help with biblical texts that preachers often ignore because of the problems they represent. We will discover that the ways such texts are handled (or rescued) are often inspired by reader response and connections with other biblical texts. They will lead us to suggest that in homiletics we need much more theoretical and methodological clarity concerning what we mean when we speak of the biblical text in the sermon.

New Approaches to the Bible in Recent Literature

A New Approach in Commentaries

Two excellent series of commentaries have recently surfaced: *The New Interpreter's Bible* and *Interpretation.*[2] The former states its purpose this way, "The general aim of *The New Interpreter's Bible* is to bring the best in contemporary biblical scholarship into the service of the church to enhance preaching, teaching, and study of the scriptures."[3] Some new commentary volumes are so fine that it is hard to restrain students in the library from preaching out loud as they read.[4] Several homileticians–many of whom are biblical scholars in their own right–have contributed to these and other series,[5] to lectionary commentaries, and preaching publications like *Journal for Preachers; Preaching: The Professional Journal for Preachers; Preaching: Word and Witness;* and *Lectionary Homiletics.*

A New Approach in Homiletical Literature

In recent decades a torrent of volumes on the Old Testament, the gospels, the epistles, and on individual Bible books have tumbled down the canyons from the publishers. Such specialized volumes are not new. For example, two decades ago D. Moody Smith of Duke Divinity School saw in form and redaction criticism new possibilities for the pulpit. Form criticism allowed preachers to see "that the Gospels are kerygmatic. That is, they are proclamation rather than biography"[6]; their rhetorical "intent and purpose" is preaching.[7] Jesus stilling the storm (Mk. 4:35–40) was originally told "to exemplify the saving work of the Lord"; in other words, Mark used the account to preach to his own community who were not on water, but from a faith perspective were in danger of sinking. Moody's suggestion is fascinating: that preachers look for the faith dimension of the text and use that to develop a bridge to today. Thus preachers today legitimately can use the Markan passage without fear of allegorizing, to preach on Jesus "rescuing storm tossed wanderers [today] and questioning their faith."[8]

One need not reject the gospels' basis in history, as Smith seems to do, to claim that the text's faith story legitimately becomes the congregation's story in the sermon by the sermon performing what the text performed. In spite of all of the recent attention to story, this faith story approach still has not been appropriated in homiletics. The closest thing to it may be in some African American preaching. There the congregation assumes the Bible story is not just about events then; it is about the congregation now. Most preaching continues to confine itself to offer the congregation only brief reflections of itself through moments of identification, rather than transcending time and reading the congregation into the biblical scene by establishing actual identity of the Bible here and now. This kind of suggestion that opens new doors for preachers in handling biblical texts is what preachers might hope to find in many of the new resources.

A New Breed of Resources

Such a flood of new books prevents us from giving more than a sampling of some of the best and most recent of them here. They constitute a new breed of critical resource separate from biblical commentaries as we know them—that is, they are not rigorous in developing historical-critical or technical issues. Rather, they are informed by these studies and presumably mediate between the critical background and the pulpit. They are selective volumes (most are around 160 pages) dealing with specialized biblical subjects and preaching. Typically they include sample sermons and strive to connect theory with practice. For example, David J. Ourisman has examined specific themes in each of the synoptic gospels. Amid his excellent analyses he contributes three very helpful questions to ask the text in producing fresh sermons:

1. Does the text *raise* a question or *answer* a question?
2. If the sermon text *raises* a question, where in the story-as-a-whole is that question answered?
3. If the sermon text *answers* a question, where in the story-as-a-whole is that question raised?"[9]

Such questions do not normally guide a preacher's reading, yet they have the potential to open new preaching possibilities.

Some of the new books have a variety of applications, including designs for various sermon series. Preachers contemplating a sermon series on a biblical book may find it very useful to have a single condensed overview as a primary resource. Among the unique features of John Holbert's *Preaching Job*[10] are direct addresses to preachers, the use of the metaphor of drama as a lens with which to appropriate the entire book of Job, and the use of a narrative preaching style for Job such that Job's experience is front and center. For Holbert, Job is a man who refuses to play the theological games of his friends, who speaks of his raw experience just as it is, and whose words even of his pain are closer to the truth than the pronouncements of his friends.[11] Holbert's advice is for preachers of Job to be bold in preaching the pain of the world and to be wary of providing easy answers about God. Holbert is faithful to his text and makes it highly accessible, yet I wonder if Job does not need to be preached in relation to its ending; otherwise, preaching Job is very close to preaching pain, and while it may be true, it is far from gospel.

Ronald J. Allen's *Preaching Luke-Acts*[12] provides exegetical helps organized according to five themes in Luke-Acts: the Realm of God; the Holy Spirit; the great reunion of the human community; restoration of women; and poverty, abundance, and the use of material resources. David Schnasa Jacobsen and Günter Wasserberg, in yet another book entitled *Preaching Luke-Acts,*[13] interpret Luke to be writing a lament for a failed mission to the Jews. They examine several texts from a post-Holocaust perspective, challenging Luke's perspective on opponents of Christ, and offer effective sermons. Each of these resources might inspire a sermon series: Allen's themes might provide a fresh perspective on Luke for a congregation accustomed to hearing individual pericopes; the other series might tie into a discussion of Jewish-Christian relations. There are possibly other advantages to such volumes over the larger commentaries written for preachers.

New Approaches to Apocalyptic Texts

Some of the volumes seem to belong to a new school of biblical-homiletical commentary that uses reader-response criticism to enter difficult texts. Biblical apocalyptic literature provides an interesting case study in the new genre of preaching books. Joseph R. Jeter and Cornish R. Rogers in 1992 anticipated that the change of the millennium would bring renewed need for preaching help with Revelation. They provide several helpful guidelines to preachers who are daring enough to listen for God's Word in John's ecstatic and imagistic terrain, not content to put the book away in a drawer labeled "awaiting more light." Jeter speaks about form: treat the symbols and images as in worship, i.e., as symbols and images instead of as propositions ("consider how the truth is painted rather than categorized").[14] If John's images no longer work today, translate or contemporize them into symbols or narratives that work. John's beast, which has no basis in reality yet communicates a feeling, may be manifested today, for example, in cancer: "utterly malevolent, powerful but cowardly, insidious, and damnably stupid—in short it has all the evil qualities of John's beast."[15] A risky hermeneutic is required for preaching Revelation. Excellent sermons, such as in the Jeter and Rogers collection, must at times become poetry in breaking open the text; postmodern criticism often blurs the distinction between the text and the reader. This will be annoying to some, who will name some of the imagery substitution eisegesis. Still, Augustine said that a figurative text cannot to be understood literally or carnally, for then it cannot edify the soul.[16]

At least two major essays on preaching apocalyptic literature were published following 1992,[17] and in 1999 two books appeared. As happens too often in homiletical literature, neither of the books builds upon or engages Jeter and Rogers. Larry Paul Jones and Jerry L. Sumney offer an excellent handbook, *Preaching Apocalyptic Texts,* that opens five texts from the Old and New Testaments. The authors try to get at the historical settings of the texts and identify several features of an apocalyptic preacher. For example, "The apocalyptic preacher believes and attempts to help others to believe that 'this is not all there is,' that there is power, goodness, and justice beyond and above that seen and experienced in the world."[18] They criticize preachers who tie apocalyptic texts to specific current events, as well as preachers who avoid preaching these texts because they do not know to what events the symbols and metaphors actually point. The texts lie beyond proof and must merely be "accepted, welcomed, and lived."[19] This book succeeds in making apocalyptic texts accessible and preachable, and partly because of the subject, God is front and center.

David Jacobsen's *Preaching in the New Creation: The Promise of New Testament Apocalyptic Texts* meets a similar need. New Testament apocalyptic texts often resist close historical-critical scrutiny and for that reason are hard to preach. Jacobsen suggests three exegetical steps:

1. Do a rhetorical analysis of the genre of the text to assess what it is trying to accomplish;

2. Determine if it moves either from divine action to cosmic convulsion and eschatological judgment, or as in Mark 13, to eschatological salvation; and

3. Do an analysis of the symbols of the text to determine whether they function to construct, maintain, or delegitimize the world.[20]

Jacobsen's exegetical suggestions are helpful and demanding. Still, one strains to hear direct discussion of his texts in his sample sermons, and they curiously operate by a different homiletic than the steps he devises for Revelation. What he does is nonetheless bold: he really does mean that preachers should not discuss the literal meaning of symbols in apocalyptic texts and instead use them in the sermon as symbols to view our world, the effect of which is similar to the text's effect. In this latter respect he is similar to Jeter and Rogers in giving preachers considerable freedom to render texts in ways that become God-centered and meaningful.[21]

New Approaches to Other Difficult Texts

The real strength of many of these volumes is they take texts like Revelation and Job that are particularly difficult to preach and explore the potential. Preachers also need help with proverbs, a genre that is often neglected because it is hard to get behind the text for material to help with preaching. Alyce M. McKenzie gives exceptional help. Her hermeneutical approach has similarities to Jacobsen's in that the center of focus in interpretation is no longer the text itself but somewhere in the space between the text and the interpreter. Preaching from as little as one line in scripture can be like dining on a bone with no meat, given the ready availability of other savory eats in the Bible. Preachers rightly ask, what has wisdom literature to do with faith? In *Preaching Proverbs: Wisdom for the Pulpit* and *Preaching Biblical Wisdom in a Self-Help Society,*[22] McKenzie answers: Wisdom is of God and signals God's presence. Wisdom sayings and principles are "condensations of an underlying, far less tidy narrative of life-experience"[23] She compares preaching proverbs to stopping at scenic outlooks where she uses the proverbs as a spotlight that searches for experiences to illuminate.[24] As she says, "Gathering a constellation of experiences to the proverb is the basic dynamic of the reading and the preaching of a proverb…"[25]

To assist this process McKenzie devises five questions that have a "narrative shape" and invite "thick description":

1. In what social setting did this wisdom arise?
2. What is most important in life according to this body of wisdom?
3. Which attitudes and actions get us closer to this vision of ultimacy?
4. What acts as obstacles to our attaining this vision of ultimacy?
5. What kind of life (Lifeform) results in living by this body of wisdom?[26]

While proverbs do not answer many historical questions we put to them, they cast light on our lives and ask to be applied to them. McKenzie's approach effectively expands the text, affording the preacher many things to say. Although the relationship of her texts to God is often assumed rather than explored and established, her sermons on proverbs often counter this.[27] Still, preachers need to ask a question beyond McKenzie's aim, How can I preach wisdom such that I preach the gospel?

Elizabeth Achtemeier wrote her *Preaching from the Minor Prophets* because of deficiencies in the lectionary: "Out of the sixty-six chapters that make up the Minor Prophets, the three year lectionary put out by the Consultation on Common Texts specifies that only twelve passages from the Minor Prophets be used for the text of the day."[28] These prophets represent three hundred years in God's plan of salvation, yet there are "few standard treatments of these texts, few performed opinions about them, few familiar ways of dealing with them." Achtemeier avoids reader response. To ensure that historical matters do not eclipse theological ones, she devotes equal time to each and then discusses sermon possibilities. She all but takes the preacher's hand into the pulpit, opens the Bible to the text, adjusts the microphone, and checks the glass of water. For Achtemeier, preaching is about God, and this small volume is one that preachers ought to have on their shelves and refer to whenever one of the minor prophets is preached. Her sketches of possible sermons reflect her own understanding that Old Testament texts need to be paired with New Testament texts to ensure the gospel is proclaimed.

Joseph R. Jeter is also concerned that preachers not ignore tough texts. Thus he has written *Preaching Judges*.[29] This is about more than the most violent book in the Bible. Jeter is a preacher's preacher, and his volume demonstrates his love of history, his knowledge of literature, his deep compassion for all who suffer, his love and reverence of God, and his holy wrestling with tough and terrible texts until they bless him. I am not always sure that the meanings he settles upon are meanings of the texts themselves, but they are meanings to which Jeter has been led by his texts in dialogue with the Christian faith, and I suspect that is a lesson he intends for us to learn.

The church from its beginning has understood that scripture interprets scripture and that the interpretation of difficult or obscure passages corresponds with what is more plainly said elsewhere. Jeter's approach is reminiscent of this. Engaging Judges is always sobering, but now it is also hopeful with gentle humor, rich stories, and wisdom that often speaks of the Divine. Perhaps something of a reader response approach is the only means whereby some texts can be preached in our day. It is not preaching a pericope, but then, preaching a pericope per se ought not to be the ultimate goal of preaching. What we are seeing in Jeter and others, for instance, with Revelation and Judges, is quite distinct from another approach of former eras when preachers found a doctrine in a text and then preached the doctrine. Whatever may be said against that approach, it typically did preach the faith and brought much of the Bible into play. This new approach is not tightly bound by the text at hand for its message, and that is perhaps a necessary loss given the nature of the text, yet this approach has similar potential to preach the faith in dialogue with tradition and other texts. It also has the potential to give God a central role.

New Approaches to the Gospels

Such an approach would not be advisable with texts that are not so difficult or terrible. A remarkable new approach with regard to the gospel of Mark is Robert Stephen Reid's *Preaching Mark*.[30] Reid is a rhetorician as well as a homiletician. He studied how chiasm and other forms of parallelism were used to structure narrative argument in ancient times, and he uses this knowledge to discern that Mark is composed of nineteen units or "narrative complexes." The clever parallelism in compositional structure that Reid identifies, the arrangement of accumulating episodes on the same theme, and the completeness of the narrative units are very persuasive. One may only wonder whether the ancients really were as clever in thinking through their narrative arguments as Reid is in analyzing them. Apart from engendering deeper respect for the ancients, Reid's work is practical. He provides preachers with a new way of preaching Mark. Reid frees preachers from the prison of pericopes by opening larger thematic or narrative units that serve the argument of the whole, and this in itself should help produce fresh sermons.

Yet another homiletician has made a unique contribution to help preachers preach from the synoptic gospels, an approach that employs what Bartlett spoke about as echoes or typologies.[31] Richard A. Jensen, perhaps inspired by Hans Frei,[32] Jack D. Kingsbury, and others,[33] was concerned that preachers often preach exegetical details from texts and thereby miss the thrust of the overarching story as well as the oral flavor. He provides a commentary that is "panoramic" and "narrative" rather than "microscopic."[34] Left-brain analysis of texts can obscure the power of biblical stories. They need simply to be retold, often accompanied by what Robert Alter called "narrative analogy" and "allusion,"[35] other similar stories from the same gospel that allow the stories to comment on each other. Thus with each text that Jensen examines, he provides a commentary on how the story at hand relates to other biblical stories. In a homiletical section he suggests how preachers might stitch together various parallel stories and situations, without explanations, allowing both the intertextual connections and the stories themselves to proclaim the gospel. An Easter sermon might tell of three related meals during which revelation occurs–Luke 9 (five loaves and two fish), Luke 22 (the last supper), and Luke 24 (Emmaus). The sermon could end with an invitation to the table where today's disciples may as surely expect to be encountered by the risen Christ as those long ago.[36] Jensen is aware of some limitations of this approach–narrative is merely a tool for preachers, not a new law.

A New Approach to Paul

A final innovative volume is Nancy Lamers Gross's *If You Cannot Preach Like Paul...*, in which she suggests that preachers ought to "Do what Paul did; don't just say what Paul said."[37] With Paul, preachers are "bringing the new reality of Christ's Lordship into an engagement with the context in which our hearers live, in order to point the way to new life in Christ."[38] Instead of thinking of Paul's letters as answers, think of them as conversations, with particular situations propelled by his urgent sense of the Lordship of Jesus.[39] Her suggestion is radical like Jacobsen's, except her Pauline text is plainly discussed in her sermons: as preachers we are imaginatively to place ourselves in the same kind of situation with Paul's same sense of urgency concerning Christ. We are to discover what we are led to say in the process of dynamic interchange with various textual conversation partners. In other words, preachers ought not to repeat Paul, but become Paul today. She hopes this is a new way to be faithful to Paul, and she queries traditional hermeneutical/homiletical models like the kernel of truth and the exegesis/bridge/application models.

The Shifting Hermeneutic

Burning Our Bridges?

Traditional hermeneutical models saw exegesis at one end of the spectrum and homiletics at the other. Gross wants to shift our understanding so that hermeneutics takes preachers through to the end of the delivered sermon, and homiletics is "the last step in the hermeneutical process."[40] Thus she finds the traditional paradigm of exegesis/bridge/application to be inappropriate, not least because it implies sequential steps.[41] She equates the bridge with interpretation and with an interpretative leap[42] –her metaphors may conflict since a bridge makes a solid connection between two bodies and a leap implies its absence. Gross's suggestion for a new paradigm is a version of the hermeneutical circle: She visualizes a swing in which the preacher is like a gymnast on a high bar, swinging between engagement of the text and engagement of various dialogue partners. The preacher swings high and low and occasionally, when enough momentum is gathered, does a giant swing over the top, moving from understanding to explanation or back.[43] Her paradigm can help preachers to see swings in their own sermon structure–times when the engagement is with the text and times when it is with dialogue partners.

I wish that Gross did not burn her bridges behind her, so to speak, for whatever deficiencies the bridge may have in implying sequenced movement, it does imply a solid connection between the text and today. One wonders what safeguards are in her approach. Since the text seems less able to provide them, they come mostly from the reader. The bridge is still useful to describe some aspects of what we do as preachers (Ricoeur taught that all metaphors have a yes and a no). In analyzing sermons it is nearly always possible and helpful to identify specific bridges, exact sentences the preacher constructs to connect the text with today. This proves true of Gross's own sermons. Often a bridge is a single idea or path, as we saw earlier in the notion of a theme sentence and especially in the transition from a MCT to a MCS. Because of the complexities of the interpretative process, it is probably best in this postmodern milieu not to seek one metaphor or paradigm that says it all. Rather the preacher should seek several that allow different things to be said, preserving those that continue to have value–bridge, bus, fluid text, spotlight (McKenzie), gymnastic swing, or whatever.

No Need for Bridges?

Gross is not the first to question the bridge metaphor. Edward Farley did so in two significant companion essays, "Preaching the Bible and Gospel," and "Toward a New Paradigm for Preaching."[44] His essays are important, for they call preachers not to think narrowly about preaching a text or unit of scripture, but to concentrate on the theological task of preaching the gospel. What preaching the gospel means cannot be reduced to specific propositions, though it has to do with good tidings of salvation through Jesus Christ: "Gospel is not a thing to be defined. It is not a doctrine, a delimited objective content. The summaries in Acts and in Paul of what is proclaimed, the formulas of the kerygma, attest to this. Phrases like the kingdom of God, Jesus as Lord, Christ crucified do have content, but that content is not simply a quantity of information."[45] It is the gospel that sets the themes of the sermon.

Farley's relatively low doctrine of scripture is one reason he challenges the bridge metaphor. He questions whether many units of scripture can bear the word of God (he means many pericopes, not just the difficult or terrible texts). One reason preaching is weak, in his opinion, is that preachers strain to find a truth in a text that does not have it and then further strain to find a bridge to apply the text to today. The ease with which he rejects many texts is worrisome for it implies that one accepts as scripture only those portions one chooses. In response one might say that perhaps the problem is in the way we read texts, more as history than as theology. The gospel and biblical texts are not the yolk and the white of an egg that are easily separated, since the identity of the gospel is only rendered in and through the texts. If one largely rejects the authority of scripture as revelation, a bridge actually becomes irrelevant—why would anyone bother to seek an analogy with the past apart from mere interest in history? Even if one is selective concerning which texts bear revelation, all bridges become suspect.

Preachers need to be humble in relation to how God uses the witness of scripture. As Calvin stressed, the Holy Spirit guides interpretation; understanding the Bible is not simply a human activity. As Barth said, "direct identification of revelation and the Bible…is not to be presupposed or anticipated by us. It takes place as an event, when and where the word of the Bible becomes God's Word…"[46] If we cannot find the word of God in a text, we should not preach it. But we ought not dismiss it as scripture or eliminate the possibility that people in some other age and circumstances—or indeed with some other notion of text or some other way of reading it—may find God's Word in it. Farley is at least a provocative stimulus to those of us in homiletics to be much more intentional about exploring and articulating just what we mean by the authority of scripture. We need to heed his call about the importance of moving beyond units of scripture to preach the gospel—all the while being more hesitant than he is to reject the bridge.

Why the Changing Nature of Resources?

We have examined only some of the recent homiletical books devoted to specific sections of the Bible. They prompt a basic question, "Why is this 'genre' appearing at this time?" The answers we give depend upon the perspective we take. Cynics may say that publishers are scrambling to fill a void. Two decades of revisions to the lectionary are over; and since the need for updated lectionary resources is reduced, new products must be found. (The release of many of the new small commentary volumes often is timed by publishers to match the rotating lectionary cycle in the church.) Other critics may peer over their eyeglasses and pronounce that preachers are less willing to work to hear a fresh word from God. A new breed of preachers has less facility or patience with the original languages, and these books provide resources that will move them quickly to homiletical reflection. Still other critics may say that scholars in homiletics face publish or perish (or publish or parish, a high calling). Homileticians find it easier to speak about the biblical texts than to discuss homiletical theory (for instance in the exemplary theoretical manner of Lucy Hogan and Richard Lischer recently on the subject of persuasion[47]). Some critics may ask why reader response seems to be stressed and why the work of biblical theologians seems not to be. These various criticism all contain a measure of truth, and homileticians who write preaching commentaries may need to be more critical, rigorous, and precise in identifying what contribution to preaching is being made and what advantage is being offered over excellent commentaries that already exist for preachers. In other words, such books would do well to engage some aspects of homiletical or hermeneutical theory that pertains to preaching and build an argument in and through the commentary.

A positive assessment of biblical publications in homiletics is also justified. One reason for the excellence of so many of the new books in preaching is that homileticians are paying attention to how preachers may both understand and control the homiletical actions in which they engage. Even though some homileticians tend to put their energies more toward the commentary end of things, they are not necessarily duplicating what others in biblical studies might be thought better equipped to do. They may fulfill a genuine need. As historical criticism improved, providing the church with more reliable texts and essential understandings about their backgrounds and meanings, biblical scholars unfortunately became more reluctant to speak about God and more willing to defer questions of truth. This new "genre" is written by teachers of preaching who are attuned both to biblical scholarship and to the needs of preachers. They intend their work to supplement other resources in sermon preparation and often open difficult or overlooked books of the Bible. They write in these directions to fulfill their commitment to preaching, not to avoid other issues. Homiletics in general may pay more attention to the biblical end of preaching than to the congregational. If there must be an imbalance, some would say that this is not a bad one to have, for it is the preachers in the field who provide the correction.

How Are These Texts Authoritative?

Homiletical scholars are making a genuine contribution in shifting the way we think about the Bible in the sermon, not just in relationship to difficult texts, texts in which it has been hard to find God's Word. Many writers we have considered are taking risks in venturing beyond the former boundaries of exegesis, even as they may be also taking 2 Timothy 3:16 seriously, "All scripture is inspired by God and is useful for teaching, for reproof, for correction, and for training in righteousness."

Sometimes in searching for a blessing in these texts, these authors engage a struggle with them that itself becomes the meaning as they bring theology, experience, and understanding to bear on these texts as well as on the rest of scripture. This implies a different notion of authority of scripture than is commonly articulated. Our view of scripture need not be the literalist one that takes all biblical texts to be of equal value, nor the fundamentalist one that insists on certain fixed ideas as absolute interpretative keys. We may affirm four key beliefs:

1. God's authority in the Word
2. the necessity of the Holy Spirit to illuminate the Word
3. the authority of the church in affirming scripture as the book by which it measures and guides its life
4. Christ's commandment that we preach the gospel

Further exploration is needed, for clearly the old boundaries between what was exegesis and eisegesis are blurred and have been for some time. Reader response criticism seems to inspire a new school of approach, as we have seen for example with Revelation and Judges. While this approach often allows the text to guide what is said, the role of God in this process is undefined. Safeguards on such interpretation require more careful articulation.

Focus on biblical texts should not obscure major issues that remain in need of discussion in homiletics that are often ignored. An example is what we mean by the biblical text in the sermon. We do not mean the biblical text itself but something rather larger to which we attach the word *text*. Were we to confine ourselves strictly to the text, we might not have very much to say, and all of our biblical commentaries are much longer than the texts themselves. We tend to appropriate to our idea of text any understanding that helps us to understand it as it would have been understood in its own time and setting, including historical, geographical, sociological, economic, archeological, and other information that we deem relevant. These items are not exactly in the text; yet we speak as though this is the text as well. Inflation of the biblical text does not stop there. We also may include our literary and theological understandings, for instance, concerning God's actions. Some scholars might see these as added on or accommodated meanings, though until relatively recently in church history, theological, not historical, meanings were assumed to be the essential text. Does our notion of text also include intertextual connections to the gospel or to parallels in other texts? Can "text" expand to include such connections to theological traditions? In other words, can we expand the literal biblical text in many ways and still call it the text, or has it become something else?

Another way of raising this question is to ask if the biblical text is ever really present in the sermon. If a biblical text is referred to in a sermon but never recreated, is it there? Even if the text is quoted word for word in the sermon, is it really the same text that is in the Bible after we have taken it out of its context of surrounding verses? Is the text actually present or do we use only a projection of the text, a re-presentation that cannot be the text itself? Perhaps we should call it a pseudo-text or an imitation of the text. Since scripture interprets scripture and we speak of the unity of scripture, can preachers ever confidently speak of a text as though it has rigid boundaries, as though the Bible itself is not the text? Or do we need a more plastic or fluid notion of text, much as we have already seen is needed when we read texts from different perspectives and get different meanings, or when we relate the text at hand to other biblical texts through certain echoes or types? We would then recognize that what we assume to be the text is an expanded understanding of it, or that the text in the sermon is altered and affected, like any object in science, by the very fact of our viewing it. I raise these issues not to split hairs, but to press for essential clarity on what we practice as preachers. Both our teaching and practice will be enriched if we are attentive to such matters— indeed some of the new commentaries could address themselves to these kinds of questions.

A God-centered Paradigm?

In this chapter we have surveyed new literature bringing new paradigms, theories, and methods to contemporary preaching in its stance toward the biblical text. We have argued for a middle ground that incorporates some new understandings and methods without totally disregarding the tried and true principles in homiletics history. Our central concern is that the authority of scripture be maintained consciously and clearly as we practice the preaching task. This means placing God firmly in the center of scripture and in our preaching.

Should homiletics in fact undergo a paradigm shift to put God at the center of scripture, it will have implications for the authority of scripture. The authority would still be rooted in the texts themselves, but the historical critical reading, once considered the preaching goal, would become only a step toward the goal. The historical critical method has never been able to account for how the word of God in a previous age is the word of God today, and that can be argued as a basic requirement for a hermeneutical method. If preaching God were placed at the center of scripture, the goal of the preacher would no longer be a fixed interpretation of a text. The preacher's aim would be to develop a fluid relationship with God who acts in particular ways in and behind the biblical text and in our world to reveal divine and human nature and to make all things new. In other words, the authority of scripture would again become the explicit authority of God to speak in the lives of the community of faith.

This can be a frightening notion, for it is easier for humans to talk about texts than it is to talk about God. Moreover, it is easier to control the interpretation of texts, difficult though this is, than it is to control the actions of a God who may be trusted to speak not just in and through the biblical text, but also in and through the gathered community who listen with the discernment of the Holy Spirit to recognize what God is saying and doing. The purpose of biblical interpretation in this perspective becomes less to render an interpretation than to be rendered by the text as it interprets our lives. (Barth said as much when he said that the interpreter is the object of the text.[48]) Instead of being conceived primarily as a rule book or answer book, in this understanding the biblical text is conceived primarily as a book of invitation to a life of risk on behalf of the neighbor and faith in a God who abundantly and graciously provides for all needs.

SECTION TWO

THEOLOGY

4

THEOLOGY OF PREACHING

The Eventful Word

What theological assumptions and understandings do we as preachers bring to preaching? How we understand what we do when we preach naturally shapes preaching practice, even as practice shapes our theology. In this chapter we will consider four vital and related emphases of contemporary theologies of preaching:

1. preaching as event;
2. the performative word;
3. preaching as transformation; and
4. preaching as poetic language and structure.

In subsequent chapters in this section we will trace the development of the trouble/grace school in homiletics that has been frequently overlooked, not only as one of the largest schools in current homiletics, but also the only one that is explicitly theological in its approach. A final chapter will examine alternative theologies of preaching.

Preaching as Event

Barth's Legacy

Our era has not put great emphasis on theologies of the word, and in some ways this is surprising. Karl Barth's entire *Church Dogmatics* arose out of his concern for preaching as God's self-revelation and for the capacity of scripture to serve as a norm for the church. One legacy we might expect from this would be a flurry of books on the word of God by his students and readers. Many volumes have appeared on this topic since the 1930s, yet not as many as one might expect. Perhaps Barth said too much, for as a systematic theologian once said (he was jesting, yet unfortunately also serious), "Barth did our theology for us; I am more interested in politics and justice." One might also have expected Lutheran homiletics, strongly rooted in theology of the Word, to maintain its former dominant influence on the North American scene, yet recently Lutheran homiletics positions have gone begging.

WORD OF GOD AS EVENT

One area of Barth's lasting influence has been on the word of God as an event of God's encounter. The concept is as old as the Bible; yet Barth put it in a preaching showcase. Martin Luther more than hinted at an event when he emphasized that in preaching Christ comes to us, and that "the gospel should really not be something written, but a spoken word."[1] John Donne likewise said, "here, in the *prayers* of the Congregation God comes to us; here, in his ordinance of *Preaching,* God delivers himselfe to us; here in the administration of his *Sacraments,* he seals, ratifies, confirmes all unto us."[2] Henry Ward Beecher, in his *Lectures on Preaching* to first year students in 1872, said something similar about what lay at the heart of ministry: "My impression is, that the fountain of strength in every Christian ministry is the power of the minister himself to realize God present, and to present him to the people."[3]

THREEFOLD WORD OF GOD

Barth identified the word of God as a threefold form:

1. the written word of God
2. the preached word of God
3. the revealed word of God[4]

For Barth, preaching rests on a commission that is beyond oneself and must simply be accepted and received; the word of God is the object of proclamation; and the Word of God alone judges proclamation to be God's Word. At the heart of these understandings is the "event" of the word of God itself, in which the human dimension of language is elevated:

[T]hrough the new robe of righteousness thrown over it, it becomes in this its earthly character a fresh event, the event of God speaking Himself in the sphere of human events, the event of Jesus Christ's vicariate plenipotentiary. Real proclamation as this new event, in which the event of human language is not set aside, but rather exalted, is the Word of God...The Word of God preached now means, in this fourth and innermost circle, man's language about God, in which and through which God Himself speaks about Himself.[5]

The Bible also becomes revelation as an event:

[D]irect identification of revelation and the Bible...takes place as an event, when and where the word of the Bible becomes God's Word, i.e. when and where the word of the Bible functions as the word of a witness, when and where John [the Baptist's] finger points not in vain but really pointedly, when and where by means of its word we also succeed in seeing and hearing what he saw and heard. Therefore, where the Word of God is an event, revelation and the Bible are one in fact.[6]

This event is not fixed or to be assumed a function of the act of preaching in itself, nor is it determined by our experience of it, but it is an act of God in and through the preaching:

We have said of Church proclamation, that from time to time it must become God's Word. And we said the same of the Bible, that it must from time to time become God's Word. Now "from time to time" had to do, not with human experience (as if our being affected by this event and our attitude to it could be as constitutive of its reality and its content!), but, of course, with the freedom of God's grace.[7]

GOD'S OTHERNESS

For Barth, the Word event is not just the act and fact of God's self-presentation through proclamation. The Word event is also the wholly Other-ness of God who nonetheless wills to become known in preaching and who, through Christ, reconciles the world to God's self. God cannot be equated simplistically with what is positive in human experience, as some had done. For Barth, the Bible has one theme: "the relation between such a God and such a man, and the relation between such a man and such a God, is for me the theme of the Bible and the essence of philosophy."[8]

Modern Response to Barth

Barth's understanding of event is important because it has influenced so much in homiletics, for good and bad. David Buttrick believes that preaching became captive to biblical theology, and he blames Barth for it. Though most of his writing was for preachers, "Barth in some ways all but destroyed preaching in the name of the Bible."[9] Barth's stress on the "objective" nature of the event of God's self-disclosure implied that preacher and contemporary experience have no role in preaching. For Barth, preaching is "from above." Buttrick maintains that denial of social relevance to the Word left preaching to be a reiteration of the biblical text–blind to the present day. Preaching has become preoccupied with "past-tense religion"[10] instead of proclaiming a present active God. "The reality of God-with-us-now is the proper focus of our preaching."[11]

Buttrick was overly hard on Barth, for if one studies his sermons, contemporary experience is very much in evidence. He corrected an anthropocentric historical critical approach to scripture in his own time, critiquing his liberal teachers who treated the Bible as though it were a mere history book. His emphasis on the eventfulness of God's Word continued, not least, with biblical scholars like Rudolph Bultmann and theologians like Gerhard Ebeling. In 1951, under the subheading of "Grace as Event,"[12] Bultmann said that grace is "not a quality"[13] of God but rather "is His now occurring act of grace"[14] in Christ's propitiatory death on the cross. God's grace is made present in the proclamation of the Word: "The salvation-occurrence is eschatological occurrence just in this fact, that it does not become a fact of the past but constantly takes place anew in the present."[15] Ebeling in 1963 spoke of the Word as an event of "participation and communication,"[16] and of the sermon as "the execution of the text,"[17] that is, as present tense proclamation of what the text proclaimed in its time.

In 1954, Donald L. Miller published his *Fire in Thy Mouth,* a volume that focused on preaching as a redemptive event.[18] He began his next book, *The Way to Biblical Preaching,* building on that understanding with the following words: "Preaching is not mere speech; it is an event. In true preaching, *something happens.* Preacher and people are brought together by the living flame of truth, as oxygen and matter are joined in living encounter by fire."[19] For him preaching is an event in which the incarnation, cross, and resurrection make up one grand event. It is this event that becomes present in preaching by turning listeners into participants:

Apart from the limitations of time and space, every life which was ever created would have been literally there gazing on Bethlehem's manger, Golgotha's agony, and the empty tomb in Joseph's garden. Through the retelling of the story, the whole event must be "placarded," re-enacted before the eyes of each successive generation, until they become living participants in both its judgment and its grace.

Only preaching which sets forth the Bible story can do this. And that which fails to do it is something other than preaching.[20]

In spite of Miller's language about story, he is not referring to narrative preaching but to traditional expository sermons about the gospel story. For Miller the objective of the preaching event is identical to the black spiritual that calls forth a yes to the question, "Were you there when they crucified my Lord?"[21] By the power of the Holy Spirit, Christ encounters listeners with judgment and redemption through proclamation of the scriptures.[22] Other scholars in the same period had notions of the eventfulness of God's Word.[23]

These notions of God's Word as event were just the beginning of the revolution that has swept homiletics in the last few decades. But before we get to that we must consider another parallel development with which it blended, which began about the same period of time, that said that language itself is eventful or performative.

The Performative Word

Partly under the influence of people outside of theology, preaching came to be seen not just as eventful but as performative: It did what it said. To some degree language itself was eventful. Literary critics like I. A. Richards from the 1930s had been arguing about the dynamic nature of metaphor as understood and pioneered by the Romantics. He turned common understanding on its head when he said that words are not like bricks or building blocks, each one equivalent to an idea. On cannot simply add them up to discover the meaning in a sentence. Rather, one must to look for "an interdependence of meanings" that recognizes that words have many meanings and many ways of achieving their purpose (rather like what we are discovering today about texts).[24] Metaphor was key in this, for it was a tensive form of language that demanded participation in order to be understood.[25] In other words, language is not a static entity.

This understanding was reinforced in 1955 by J. L. Austin, who lectured at Harvard University on the subject, *How to Do Things with*

Words. He spoke of "a performative sentence or a performative utterance...The term 'performative'...indicates that the issuing of utterance is the performance of an action."[26] Obvious examples of performative utterance include saying "I promise," by which one commits oneself to a course of action, or a minister saying, "I pronounce you husband and wife," by which the couple are wed. Austin was thinking of particular kinds of speech, but the term "performative" also was seen to characterize God's Word and became attached to discussions of event. In this view, the effectiveness of preaching cannot rest in the number of people who hear it, or in a preacher's ability to perform it, but in God's ability to bring about what is spoken. As Isaiah 55:11 says, "so shall my word be that goes out from my mouth; / it shall not return to me empty, / but it shall accomplish that which I purpose, / and succeed in the thing for which I sent it."

The New Hermeneutic

The eventful nature of God's Word and the performative nature of metaphor and language came together in *The New Hermeneutic* (1964) with scholars like Ernst Fuchs and Gerhard Ebeling. They promoted the idea of the "language event" or "word event": Preaching participates in God's word-event. Through preaching Jesus' living word is an event today.[27] In the preaching of Christ, Christ is present; in participation in the words, Christ is encountered; in the reception of him, life is transformed, people receive their lives anew. Paul Scherer, who taught preaching at Union Seminary in New York, placed similar emphasis on event in 1965. The Bible is concerned, he said, "first and foremost with the mighty and saving acts of God."[28] Isaiah and Jeremiah not only tell of what God has done and will do, "they are heralds of a Word which itself fashions the event."[29] In the act of preaching, God "is not intent on sharing conceptual truth. That must come later. It is not some saving measure of information he wants to impart; it is himself he wants to bestow: that not having seen him we may yet meet him."[30] Revelation for Scherer is always a transformative event, for God's words perform what they say: "God kept on talking...after his book went to press. His word may be something spoken or something done. He says by doing, and he does by saying. Events become words."[31]

David Randolph[32] and Charles Rice[33] separately argued that the Word encounters us as an event of God that performs things, and preaching should facilitate that encounter. As a result of these and other influences, homiletics started to turn to narrative and plot to reflect the way people experience life and God, and away from abstract propositions or points. Jesus' own parables served as a model. Essential though structure is, the original strength of the narrative movement was its theological ability to generate experience through which God might be perceived.

A Critical Perspective

We do not need to loose the hounds to sniff out every recent path taken by preaching as a performative event, for the history of research has largely been done already.[34] Significant criticism of preaching as event has also been raised. Lucy Rose finds too grand the idea that every sermon will be an encounter between God and the individual soul.[35] She holds out the possibility that something else may be happening when faith does not seem to be addressed in preaching, though she is not clear on what this is.[36] She may overstate her case when she says that "language is also limited and participates in the sins and distortions of the generations and cultures that use and reshape it...The claim that all language is irrevocably biased precludes the preacher's discovering an intention, voice, or experience that purports to be the text's intention, the voice of God, or a paradigmatic gospel experience."[37] If she really means that scripture is no longer capable of bearing revelation, there would seem to be little purpose in preaching or in the church.

Richard Lischer identifies two kinds of preaching as event, both of which he finds deficient. In preaching-from-above, "The truth of the Word cannot be affected in any way by the formal characteristics of its language conveyance. Indeed Barth argued that the form of the sermon served only to obscure the Word of God."[38] A more general theology of revelation informs preaching-from-below, "Scratch deeply enough into ordinary experience and you will discover intimations of or analogies to the divine life. According to this view, the Bible's only purpose is to provide the clues where to scratch."[39] Both are events, one "mediates an experience of God on *God's* terms" while the other "does the same but on *human* terms."[40] The problem with both is excessive individualism; they are inattentive to the church. "The Word falls on the conscience of the individual but does not render or inform the life of the community."[41] Instead of event, Lischer prefers the image of a pilgrimage or journey, for this fosters an understanding of the need for moral formation and community formation required of God's people in the world.[42] His new image retains an eventful character nonetheless.

In speaking of preaching as an event, we mean not only that it is an event because words are eventful, but also that it is an event because

God comes to us in power in and through the proclamation of God's Word to accomplish what is spoken. Preaching is not just information about God, or communication in God's name, it is about the bestowal of God's power and the reception of God's grace. Preaching as event represents a considerable degree of consensus in preaching today. We may now focus on three offshoots of event and performance in homiletics: preaching as transformation; preaching as poetic language and structure; and, in the next two chapters, we will examine further influence of performative event when we consider preaching as theological structure.

Preaching as Transformation

The term "transformational preaching" has gained some currency, not least because of the work of people like Richard A. Jensen[43] and more recently Lucy Rose and David Brown.[44] Others have referred to transformational preaching as narrative, imaginative, or existential preaching; and yet none of these terms is a precise synonym. Rose prefers transformative because "it conveys the commonly held belief that the sermons should be an experience that transforms the worshippers."[45] Still, to some people this term may seem presumptuous, as though the congregation is made up of dedicated backsliders who need radical change each week. We use the term to speak of what is effected through preaching, lives are transformed and conformed to the image of Christ.

Preaching to Make a Difference

All preaching tries to make a difference in people's lives. That is why Christ commissioned people to do it. Many years ago, W. E. Sangster said, "Nothing is more foolish...than the supposition that preaching does not *do* anything. Preaching is a constant agent of the divine power by which the greatest miracle God ever works is wrought and wrought again. God uses it *to change lives.*"[46] Richard Lischer's image of a community journey or pilgrimage is a good antidote to thinking that all God does is to effect individual transformation: "*preaching,* as opposed to individual sermons, forms a community of faith over time."[47] The purpose of preaching is the moral transformation of the entire church into a caring community in the image of Christ.

In many churches a sermon is conceived as primarily information rather than as transformation or formation, and its purpose is to be received, understood, accepted, and remembered. The preacher's role is often that of a teacher or lecturer imparting knowledge. Still, even in this informational model, something happens in preaching, whether it be teaching, moving people to laughter or tears, or calling for a moral or faith decision. Thus when we contrast informational with transformational preaching, we speak of something that is *relatively* static as opposed to a more dynamic event.

For Rose, transformational preaching opens a new way of seeing oneself, one's neighbors, and the world.[48] However, as she explains what she means by transformational preaching, it is clear that Rose means something rather less than what others may intend. For her it is preaching that de-emphasizes God: Instead of developing "an encounter with God" it "emphasizes more the preacher's responsibility in the sermon's becoming an event."[49] The sermon apparently no longer "mediates God and knowledge of God through divine self-revelation. In transformational views of preaching the dominant focus shifts to the human side of the encounter."[50] Such preaching addresses ideas, yet it also assists listener participation. In response to Rose, many homileticians would have a difficult time separating God's action from the transformative part of preaching. If the goal of preaching is to be simply transformative, there is little to mark as unique to the church, little to separate what it does from manipulation by ideology or some other means. Preaching presumably is transformative because God uses it for formation: to form listeners as disciples of Christ and to unite them as his body, the church. It is not just the faith formation of individuals that occurs, it is the formation of a community of service.

Theologically, the power and efficacy of what most people think of as transformative preaching comes from the fact that God's Word is spoken, not some other word. As John Stott says, citing Isaiah, "*God's Word is powerful.* For not only has God spoken; not only does God continue to speak through what he has spoken; but when God speaks he also acts. His Word does more than explain his action; it is active in itself."[51] All of this is to say that as preachers we do the best that we can to facilitate the transforming work of the Holy Spirit. The power of the sermon to transform people's lives still has more to do with God and faith than it has to do with how preachers do what they do.

Preaching and Systematic Theology

Gerhard O. Forde identifies another dimension of transformational preaching, a moment of what he calls proclamation within the larger act of preaching. In his *Theology Is for Proclamation* he gives a systematic theologian's assessment of what is needed from the pulpit. What he calls proclamation is unheard, that is, the present tense unconditional declaration of good news "authorized by what occurs in Jesus Christ according to the scriptures."[52] Proclamation is performative: It "is not 'about' something other than itself. It does not point away from itself. It does not signify some other thing. It is the saying and doing of the deed itself, for example, 'I baptize you.'"[53] Once this Word is appropriately set forth in the congregation it accomplishes its purpose. He says proclamation is unheard, the present-tense unconditional declaration of good news *from* God, a Word of love set loose in the midst of the congregation to achieve its purpose. What we too often have in the pulpit instead, says Forde, is Systematic theology, secondary abstract past-tense discourse reflection *about* God, "albeit systematics of a second-rate or rather unsystematic sort."[54] He advocates recovery of the proper correlation of the two: Systematics clarifies and gives order to abstract thought but must inevitably *lead to* proclamation, for it is the assent of faith, not of reason, which is the ultimate persuasion; proclamation will present a radical discontinuity between Jesus who puts to death the old ways and Jesus who calls us into new life.

Preaching Leading to Action

Richard A. Jensen shares Forde's understanding of proclamation, which he identifies as first or second person present tense language spoken on Christ's behalf: "This kind of proclamation is worlds removed from preaching that only explains what it was that Christ said and did at some point in the past. Understanding is not the goal. Proclamation is the goal. How that proclamation works itself out in the lives of people is the work of the Holy Spirit."[55] He points to a further dimension of transformational preaching: It leads to faith and trust in God. For Jensen,

> Faith almost always gets its shape in dependence on our understanding of the Word of God. If God's Word is basically understood as a book containing all the truths about God, faith is understood as belief in those truths. If God's Word is understood to be that book which tells us all about Jesus and his love, faith is that human activity which chooses to believe in Jesus and his love. If the Word of God is understood to be an oral, creative word which creates what it announces, faith is understood to be a living trust that what that Word has announced to us is the new reality of our life.[56]

The stories of preaching should not be *metaphors of illustration,* illustrating points already made. The stories of preaching should be *metaphors of participation,* involving listeners in their world, offering an experience.[57]

In summary, preaching is transformational because this is what it means to have a relationship with the Divine who is for us: Individuals are restored to what God intended, and communities are shaped and empowered for discipleship. Transformation may be something that preachers can assist, but it is God's activity that is transformative. Such is the nature of God who encounters hearers in and through the proclaimed Word with life-changing power that makes saints out of sinners, and new creations out of the old.

Preaching as Poetic Language and Structure

We have been considering three related categories in homiletics: preaching as event, as performative, and as transformational. We now move to a different kind of category, preaching as poetics, to consider how God's Word as event led to a change in how the sermon is structured and how theology is done in preaching. Language shifted away from logic, argument, points, and illustrations toward poetry, imagination, metaphor, and story. H. Grady Davis introduced this change. His brilliant and groundbreaking *Design for Preaching* (1958)[58] is possibly the most significant book in homiletics of the last century, even ahead of Craddock's *As One Without Authority.*[59]

Preaching and the Language of the Romantics

Samuel Taylor Coleridge and William Wordsworth are two Romantics who were instrumental in revolutionizing how our world thinks about art and language. Davis seems to have been the first person since Horace Bushnell (1802–1876) and Frederick W. Robertson (1816–1853)[60]–both within the first wave of Romantic influence–to bring insights from the Romantics and the arts to bear significantly on homiletics. Following are key ideas of the Romantics:

1. Organic as opposed to predetermined form. Poetry has a life of its own and each poem operates by its own rules or hidden dynamics that give it unity and meaning.

2. The importance of imagination. For Coleridge imagination was the highest faculty, even above reason, for it allowed perception of truth through the reconciliation of opposites and generation of new meaning.

3. Metaphor as a tensive language that says things in its own unique ways. Metaphor is not simply a decoration in language that can be discarded, and other words cannot be substituted

to say more plainly what it says. It has the ability to evoke feelings and to say things beyond the literal and material.

4. The eventful nature of art in bringing new reality into being. Art not only represents and describes things, it creates new things and offers new experiences that do not depend on representation of existing reality.

5. Language as an instrument that shapes consciousness and affects how the world is perceived. Words are not just tools that consciousness uses to shape understandings, rather, words shape consciousness and without them we would not be able to perceive the world as we do.

In the 1930s, I. A. Richards, mentioned earlier, reintroduced Coleridge's ideas of metaphor, poetic form and function, and primary and secondary imagination to the academic community, thus beginning the second wave of Romantic influence.[61] The Romantics had rejected classical set forms of poetry and art into which one poured a certain content, and they favored instead forms arising out of the content that were influenced by imagination and emotion. Metaphor became central in their understanding of language because of its ability to evoke feelings and to address things beyond the senses.

In the 1950s, Davis similarly critiqued rigid sermon forms that he called nonfunctional sermon forms (e.g., three points) that simply fit a style but had no connection with the purposes of the sermon. He defined the functional form of a sermon as "the form that sermon takes the better to accomplish the definite purpose for which it is preached."[62] He innovated organic forms that exhibit growth, valued emotion, and sought language appropriate to the oral medium. As he said, "it remains a fact that too little use is made of narrative in contemporary preaching."[63] He compared the sermon to a tree. Instead of a number of mechanical points, it was to have "one sturdy thought like a single stem / With natural limbs reaching up to light." Its sentences were to be "like leaves native to this very branch." Its illustrations were to open "from inside these very twigs," not as "brightly colored kites / Pulled from the wind of someone else's thought / entangled in these branches."[64] Davis knew he was proposing something new. He warned his readers concerning organic forms, "I fear you will not find much help in the literature of preaching on the problems of this chapter."[65]

Davis's significance for theology in preaching has not been widely noticed, perhaps because his significance does not arise out of his explicit theology of preaching, on which his comments are brief yet pointed. Nonetheless, he understood preaching to be an encounter with God in Christ. He used the word *proclamation* as Forde and Jensen used it. Proclamation "must take the form of an offer of life–not merely the messenger's offer in God's name, but God's offer made directly and personally to the hearer, an offer of life from the Source of life...not a promise concerning God, but a promise made by God."[66] Davis's significance has to do with how theology is done in the sermon.

Davis knew that organic and formalist thought from the Romantics had reshaped the study of English literature. In a bold and decisive move, he applied it to preaching. Davis connected the sermon with what Barth and others were saying about event. Good Lutheran and poet that he was, Davis saw a link between being encountered by God in the sermon and designing the sermon so that that encounter was facilitated and experienced in it. Since Christ is the living Word, the sermon should demonstrate organic life, each sermon appropriate to its message, each form affected by its text. Texts should not just be attached to sermons; they should be their living source.[67] The event of the Word affected both theological expression and sermonic structure.

Davis's Contributions to Preaching

Other scholars would hoe and water the ground Davis tilled and planted. They would extend the implications of his thought. Still, his book was ahead of its time in using

1. his own poetry to communicate the poetic dimensions of sermon form and language[68]
2. dramatic dialogue as a means of teaching[69]
3. the examples of novelists, dramatists, artists, and poets as models for preachers
4. the model of narrative sermons

He also identified potential weaknesses in using narrative.[70] He said, "[W]e preachers forget that the gospel itself is for the most part a simple narrative of persons, places, happenings, and conversation. It is not a verbal exposition of general ideas."[71] He spoke of the sermon in revolutionary ways based in the arts:

> The proper design of a sermon is a movement in time. It begins at a given moment, it ends at a given moment, and it moves through the intervening moments one after another...A sermon is not a manuscript, not a paper outline simple or elaborate, not a sketch like one of those in this

book...A sermon is not static like a painting...[It] never has the objective completeness of a picture or building. A sermon is like music, not music in the score but in the live performance, where bar is heard after bar, theme after theme, and never all at once. A sermon is like a play, not the printed book but the action on a stage, which moves from a first act through a second to a third, and the drama is never seen all at once. A sermon is like a story told aloud, where each sentence has gone forever into the past before the next is spoken. If we wish to learn from other arts, we must learn from these arts based on a time sequence.[72]

In other words, Davis was both demonstrating and advocating that theology could be communicated in other than strictly propositional ways. Parts contribute to the whole; the whole is affected by each of its parts; and anything that does not function for the organic unity of the whole should be removed. The shape of the whole is influenced by the contents and rhetorical purpose of the biblical text. As a result of Davis, further varieties of sermon form begin to emerge. Art and artists become models for preachers expressing theological truths. Deductive preaching that proves a point becomes seen as only one way of preaching; inductive preaching becomes possible (first ventured as a theoretical possibility by W. E. Sangster in 1954[73]) that explores experience and narrows to a focus. Such understandings may seem obvious today, but in Davis's time this was unbroken ground in new territory. In the next two chapters we move to consider one of the most extensive impacts of preaching as event, namely preaching as theological structure.

5

THEOLOGICAL STRUCTURE I

Law and Gospel

In the next two chapters we discuss perhaps the most significant implication for preaching as event, namely theological structure. We saw earlier with regard to biblical texts how their form and rhetorical purpose has a significant impact on how they are interpreted for preaching. We now will see that sermon form has been discovered to have a significant impact on their theological content and outcome.

Traditional Separation of Form and Theology

H. Grady Davis believed that a mechanical approach to sermon form left much to be desired because content and form affected each other. Up to then, homileticians typically saw the structure of the sermon as something mechanical and separate from its theology. A preacher chose a form and poured theology into it as content, much like making ice cubes or concrete blocks. An expository sermon moved from the exposition of a biblical text to its application today. A topical sermon might move up a ladder of points of increasing significance or, around an issue, as one might examine the many facets of a diamond. The theological purpose of the sermon was largely independent of form. The purpose of an exegetical sermon might be to expound a certain text verse by verse, while the purpose of a doctrinal sermon might be to explain a doctrine.

Theology and function were thought to be separate and distinct. Apart from choice of a sermon form, the main thought given to structure had to do with the logical order of points and sub-points and with rhetorical sequencing of ideas, so that, for example, the strongest point came last, the second strongest came first, and the weakest came in between. All of this came about without ever asking, How does form affect the theology that is preached? Preachers generally felt that sermons could import systematic theology directly into the sermon without having to pay customs duty. Thus, a theological essay could be imported to the pulpit without significant alteration and still be called a doctrinal sermon. Some North American and many contemporary European sermons sound like this to our ears. The form of the sermon provides no assistance for the preacher as a pastor or as a theologian talking about God.

Theology as a Way of Structuring Sermons

Once homileticians became aware that the content of sermons was affected by form, they began looking for ways to allow the sermon's rhetorical purpose to influence its shape and structure. They asked a vital question: If the sermon were to bring people into a relationship with God and not just knowledge about God, then ought not the sermon be structured to facilitate that relationship? They began looking for guidance to an age-old theological issue. From the time of the early church, and then again with Luther, two theological categories–law and gospel–have been lurking around the pulpit with important connection to preaching. Paul wrestled with them in particular in Romans. Augustine identified law and grace as one of the few kinds of theological senses or meanings to be found in any scriptural passage.[1] The full implications of these terms for preaching were never fully explored, even with Luther. In a moment we will see how they have evolved, especially in the last 150 years, from categories in Lutheran theology to fruitful homiletical principles of form and function in circles far beyond the Lutheran tradition.

The Law and Gospel Tradition

Ask many homileticians about law and gospel, and they will give two typical answers: (1) law and gospel is a sermon form favored by Lutherans, and (2) it moves from law to gospel. Most homileticians would be surprised to discover that both answers are wrong. Lutheran homiletics never taught this, at least in published form.[2] Only recently has law and gospel become an overall sermon movement, initially under the influence of an *Episcopalian,* not a Lutheran. People from various denominations developed it, as we will see. Though it goes largely unnoticed, law and gospel (or what we will call trouble and grace) has become a major school of homiletical thought.

LUTHER'S INFLUENCE

In 1532 Luther preached law and gospel as basic to the principles of the Protestant reformation. One of his sermons introduces us to his meaning:

> Consequently we must now learn to distinguish between the two parts which are called the law and the gospel...The law brings us before the judgment seat, for it demands that we must be good and love out of a pure heart and a good conscience...But we teach that one should know and look upon Christ as the one who sits there as the advocate of the poor, terrified conscience; believe in him, not as a judge, who is angry and ready to punish, but as a gracious, kindly, comforting mediator.[3]

Luther was not talking about homiletical methodology here or in numerous other places where he speaks on this subject. Rather, he discussed the content of the gospel message and of dividing the biblical writings so as to discern the word of God. Early in his priesthood he mistakenly associated law with the Old Testament and gospel with the New. Only later did he recognize that law and gospel are two different kinds of emphasis or weight within the single unity of the Word, whether Old or New Testament. Because Luther had fallen into this error, others following him like lemmings fell into it as well. This created one of the profound problems with law and gospel in preaching: Some preachers assumed that it is appropriate to preach judgment from the Old Testament and then switch to the New Testament to find the good news. Moreover, because Luther made this mistake, many preachers think that use of law and gospel today still implies his error. These simplistic and lingering notions have done much to prevent the kind of good preaching Luther sought and modeled in his later years and have hindered many preachers from receiving and using a highly effect theological approach.

WILLIAM PERKINS AND JOHN WESLEY

Others beyond Lutheran circles discovered intuitively or otherwise the usefulness of law and gospel as a means of doing theological reflection. The great Church of England Puritan theologian, William Perkins, in his homiletical text, *The Arte of*

Prophecying (Latin, 1592; English, 1607), identified law and gospel as "the basic principle" in applying biblical doctrines to contemporary life: "The law exposes the disease of sin, and as a side-effect stimulates and stirs it up. But it provides no remedy for it. However the gospel not only teaches us what is to be done, it also has the power of the Holy Spirit joined to it. When we are regenerated by him we receive the strength we need both to believe the gospel and to do what it commands."[4] He saw a natural order in them: "The law is, therefore, first in the order of teaching; then comes the gospel."[5]

In 1751, John Wesley was concerned with teaching his followers to preach Christ, and law and gospel were central to his approach. He called them, "the scriptural way, the Methodist way, the true way."[6] Some preachers in Wesley's society were said to preach one or the other. Wesley opposed them as unfaithful in their preaching. Law and gospel are to be juxtaposed, yet for him they do not constitute a methodology for preaching; as for Luther, they are a way of reflecting theologically. Wesley said they could be preached "in their turns," mixing them "both at once, or both in one."[7] His own sermons move back and forth between law and gospel with no apparent plan or structural benefit from the terms.[8]

C. F. W. WALTHERS

We jump now to one of the foremost interpreters of Luther on these matters, Professor C. F. W. Walthers at Concordia Seminary in St. Louis, Missouri, during the 1880s. He often devoted his Friday evenings to informal lectures, beyond those he gave during the week to his regular classes. This enabled him to speak to the German-American public and, perhaps of equally great advantage, to provide more edifying evenings for his students than they were likely to find seeking weekend entertainment downtown on their own. We do not know with what gladness they filed into the auditorium on those nights.

During one series, from September 12, 1884, to November 6, 1885, Walthers devoted thirty-nine lectures to interpreting Luther on the subject of *The Proper Distinction Between Law and Gospel.* These lectures were published posthumously in German in 1897 from a student's stenographic notes.[9] Walthers chose the topic because the 1577 Lutheran confession, the Formula of Concord, had stated that law and gospel were necessary to understand scripture correctly. Law and gospel, he said, are a means to bring people to conversion: Law addresses the conscience and discloses an individual's sin. Without law written in the heart, the gospel cannot be heard. The law exists as a threat; as with Abraham and Hagar, it "hands us a piece of bread and drives us out into the desert."[10] The gospel, by contrast, "demands nothing at all" but "invit[es] a hungry person to come to the table to eat...to partake of heavenly blessings."[11] "The Law tells us what we must do, while the Gospel speaks only of what God does."[12]

For Walthers, law and gospel are to be preached to different people. His understanding is mechanical. Law produces a guilty conscience, contrition, fear, and confession. Law should be preached to people who are confident in their sin, while gospel should be preached to terrified sinners. Gospel functions like the father of the prodigal son: "[T]he father does not in a single word refer to the son's dreadful and disgraceful conduct; he says nothing, nothing about that, but simply embraces and kisses the prodigal and prepares a splendid banquet for him...[Gospel] issues no commands, but it transforms man, implants love in his heart, and equips him for all good works."[13]

Law and gospel must be preached in such a way that the hearer is in no doubt as to whom each of these addresses. There was no order or overall movement to law and gospel. Hearers ought not to assume that all is well because a sermon might move from law in one part to gospel in another: "Such a topographical division is meaningless. Both may be contained in the same sentence, but every hearer must be able to say, 'That is meant for me!'"[14] In private one must not proclaim the gospel to an unrepentant sinner, for it can do that person no good; but in the sermon, even though some impenitent people are present, both must be proclaimed. The penitent person must be able to hear a word of comfort and think, "Oh, that is a sweet word! That's for me."[15] Walthers instructed his preaching students to separate law and gospel, and not mix them up so that no one understands what applies to whom. He calls this separation the "ultimate test of a proper sermon."[16]

Law and gospel exist primarily as distinct and opposing repeated emphases in a sermon. Nowhere in Walthers do they represent an overall movement or flow in the sermon from law to gospel. He discussed the pair as elements of theological argument, acknowledging that within a sermon each may frequently appear. Some individuals may be able to appropriate both: "First the Law must perform its office so that the hearers, starving and parched, will receive the Gospel in big gulps."[17] Luther's sermons may have little appeal at first, but Walthers makes them sound fun, like a trip to a roller coaster at the fairgrounds. On every sermon page,

> First he scares the living daylights out of you and hurls you down into the depths. But he has hardly done that when he

says, "Do you believe that?" "Yes." "Good, come back up!"
There is thunder and lightning, but then immediately the
gentle breath of the Holy Spirit in the Gospel. It is impossible
to resist... He constantly preaches Law and Gospel side by
side, so that the Law is illustrated in a far more terrifying
way by the Gospel, and the Gospel is made far sweeter and
more consoling through the Law."[18]

Johann Michael Reu

The idea of law and gospel was not confined to Lutheran circles.
It is unlikely that C. H. Spurgeon would have heard of Walthers. Still
Spurgeon taught that a sermon that does not offer the grace of God is
a failure: "[I]t sweeps over men's heads like a cloud, but it distributes
no rain upon the thirsty earth; and therefore the remembrance of it
to souls taught wisdom by an experience of pressing need is one of
disappointment, or worse."[19]

One Lutheran who knew Walther's writings well was Johann
Michael Reu, who taught homiletics at Wartburg Seminary in
Dubuque, Iowa, some years after Walther's death in 1887. Reu
approvingly cites Walthers at length in his *Homiletics* (1922).[20] Reu is
best known for his detailed melding of German and North American
homiletical scholarship and for his advocacy of the importance of
exegetical method. He coined a phrase that we should remember, if
not to amuse then to instruct us: "the exegetical conscience of the
preacher." As he explained, "The more sharply a truth has been
defined in the exposition of the text, the more completely will the
exegetical conscience of the preacher be satisfied."[21] Reu speaks of
law and gospel again as mechanical, propositional kinds of content
within theology itself. He gives helpful definitions of each: "Law...is
whatever declares the mandatory or punitive will of God; whatever
commands or prohibits, uncovers sin, judges, punishes, [or]
condemns...Gospel, on the other hand, is whatever declares the
gracious and saving will of God; whatever promises, proclaims,
communicates God's grace, justifies and saves–whether it come from
the Old or the New Testament..."[22] Reu, as Walthers, sees some
movement between law and gospel but no overall sermon movement
dictated by these terms. While law and gospel may be found in the
same Bible passage,[23] and while only the Holy Spirit can rightly divide
the two,[24] the preacher's task is to determine, according to the spiritual
needs of the congregation, which of the two to preach.[25] Overall
sermon movement is linear, logical, and classically rhetorical, such
that the preacher, "is never found making any step, in any direction,

which does not advance his main object, and lead towards the conclusion to which he is striving to bring his hearers."[26] He outlines numerous sermons by their main points, as Walthers had done.[27] Again in Reu law and gospel do not direct the overall argument. One sermon example proceeds with each point as a gospel/law: The church alone possesses: (1) "the treasure of forgiveness: have you made this treasure your own?"; (2) "the true knowledge of God: have you this knowledge to your soul's salvation?"(3) "complete obedience to God's will: are you rendering God this obedience?"[28]

KARL BARTH

Following Reu, two non-Lutherans entered the discussion. In 1935, when Karl Barth was dismissed from Bonn University for failing to take the oath of allegiance to Adolf Hitler, he wrote a paper entitled "Gospel and Law." He claimed that the proper order was gospel-law-gospel. Barth, too, was not creating a pattern for sermon development, although homiletical writers sometimes mistakenly project that onto him.[29] Instead, he was talking in thinly veiled terms about the need for the Confessional Church to conceive of law as an ethical *response* to the gospel and of the church's need to be willing to sacrifice for the unjustly persecuted, instead of merely praying for them. The law of the Third Reich was a perversion of the law. To know Christ is to do his will.[30] The law, appropriately understood, "is nothing less than the necessary form of the Gospel, whose content is grace," just as grace becomes "the summons to grace" (i.e., law), meaning "the Church which dares must dare to speak with authority."[31] In other words, the gospel must give shape to the nation's law that must in turn lead to the gospel, hence his order gospel-law-gospel.

H. H. FARMER

Congregationalist H. H. Farmer used analogous terms in 1942 when he suggested that the master text of all sermons is, "Behold I stand at the door and *knock*." Too many sermons, he said, make no claim or summons to do God's will. Listening to such sermons is like being in a hotel and hearing someone moving around: "They begin, they trickle on, they stop, like the turning on and turning off a tap behind which there is no head of water."[32] One may hear very true statements, but none of them present a knock at the door. "At best there has been only the rustle of someone's skirts passing the door."[33]

Farmer suggests that preachers place an additional motto above their desks, "Please do not knock if an answer is not required."[34] He adds, "I do not believe that God ever comes lovingly to a man or woman without making a claim, a demand [i.e., law]. Nor does He ever come without proffering strength and succour [i.e., gospel]. The two, the demand and the succour, are inseparable."[35] Each must be found simultaneously in the same word: "God's demand is His succour, and His succour is His demand. 'My meat is to do the will of Him that sent me.' The meat is not added as a reward for doing the will."[36] For Farmer any homiletical attempt to separate or distinguish law and gospel is inappropriate. When they are separated, no demand is made: "I shrink therefore from any tendency to separate and set in antithesis to one another gospel and demand…the element of claim must never be absent from your preaching. It must not in principle even be subordinate. It must be part of the gospel, part of comfort. For, I repeat, in the end without God's claim gospel is not gospel and comfort does not comfort."[37]

Farmer, on the one hand, advocates law and gospel as essential every time we preach. On the other hand, Farmer curtails the ability of law and gospel to function as homiletical guidelines, for if they must be experienced simultaneously as claim and succor there is little a preacher can do by way of ensuring their presence or separating them for theological and rhetorical purpose. From this perspective, William Perkins was more advanced.

Nearly forty years later Lutheran homiletician Morris J. Niedenthal supported Farmer's idea of preaching both claim and succor simultaneously.[38] Niedenthal helpfully interpreted the grammar of law as the conditional, "If A, then B;" in contrast to the declarative grammar of gospel, "Because A, therefore B." In other words, both law and gospel have an imperative that allows each to be heard in the other, but where the law "presupposes strength but does nothing to create it,"[39] the gospel "seeks to create [strength] by ministering to need and weakness."[40]

H. GRADY DAVIS

In the 1950s two writers from separate Lutheran traditions each indicated that in their own thinking, law and gospel were starting to become more than just two emphases of God's Word. H. Grady Davis was the first writer in homiletics to hint at law and gospel as an overall sermon movement. That he took this role is not surprising. As seen in our previous chapter, the organic development of a sermon led him not only to speak of how a sermon "grows," but also of how law and gospel represent a flow that can determine sermon shape. He referred to a sermon he heard preached on the text: "Apart from me you can do nothing."

The preacher's whole emphasis is that of ourselves we can neither gain God's consideration, deserve it, nor believe in it...The sermon's falseness is not that it points out our helplessness to help ourselves but that it stops with saying this, as if it were the whole truth about our situation, or even the important truth.[41]

Rather, Davis implied a development of the gospel from the center of the sermon:

The apprentice must learn to make sure that the gospel is in his germinal idea to begin with. If it is not there, it cannot be at the heart of the sermon where it ought to be. The gospel cannot successfully be dragged in later. The last point of the sermon is much too late to begin thinking about the gospel.[42]

This brief comment seems to be the first recorded suggestion of an organic treatment of law and gospel, one that found in their dynamic relationship a possible structure to govern the movement of sermon form toward the purpose of proclamation.

RICHARD R. CAEMMERER

One year later, in 1959, Richard R. Caemmerer of Concordia Seminary came close to but stopped short of prescribing movement from one to the other. For him the law is not genuine preaching. It "is always God's saying: 'You are cutting yourself off from Me, you are experimenting with death; see its signs! You need help!'"[43] He cautioned preachers not to think that their final purpose is accomplished "when people begin to dissolve in sorrow over their sins or anxiety over their grief."[44] The preacher "sounds the alert [of law] simply that the people might pick up their ears and stand with their hands outstretched, saying: 'Very well, preacher, tell us again how God rescues us.' Then the 'preaching,' the telling of the good news, really begins."[45]

Caemmerer is best known for his three-stage development of the sermon: goal, malady, and means. After determining what the text is about (i.e., the theme sentence), the preacher begins by identifying the *goal* of the sermon, a succinct statement of what the preacher wants to persuade the listener in terms of an improvement in faith or life as suggested by the text. The goal is not the preacher's goal. It is God's goal for the listener. Typically this involves repentance or a summons to repentance and belief.[46] The *malady* is God's judgment that offers a diagnosis of what is wrong. It concerns the death humans choose for themselves separate from God, God's wrath or withdrawal, and God's judgment of sin.[47] The malady is the "opposite" of the goal. (As an example in Jn. 3:16, "That my hearer may more thoroughly understand how to be saved" is the goal that leads to the malady, "[The hearer] does not understand how to be saved.")[48] The *means* is the "obverse" of the malady[49] and is a proclamation of God's grace or rescue as it is found in the immediate text at hand or in the larger section of scripture.[50]

Goal, malady, and means represent a rhetorical strategy for persuasive design that facilitates preaching the Word of the cross.[51] However, they are not to be conceived as an overall movement from law (goal and malady) to gospel (means):

> Isn't it true that the accent on persuasion...will suggest the major division for every text: I. Goal, II. Malady, III. Means? No...that division [is] possible only where the text discusses all three. Even then, it may not be preferable, for that division tends to slot all of the affirmation of the Gospel into one section. When the preacher can confront his hearers with Law and Gospel repeatedly in the same sermon without muddling his plan, then he is on the track of a good outline.[52]

Although they are developing in this direction, in Caemmerer law and gospel are not yet the dynamic factors that they will become in homiletical theory, generating in the tension between themselves the overall movement of the sermon. Rather, goal, malady, and means are still a way for the preacher to ensure that the text adequately speaks through a sermon to determine its content.

That Caemmerer's book is still in print by Concordia Publishing House is a tribute to its significance, at least in Missouri Synod circles. Some of his understandings of law and gospel now seem limited or dated. This is not the static law and gospel we saw earlier, for goal, malady, and means imply progression and order; yet this progression is rhetorical. Sermon structure is a mechanical outline of points, and law and gospel have little impact on it[53] except somehow to "cue" goal, malady, and means.[54] His goal of getting people "to understand" may seem too exclusively intellectual an appeal. Like those before him, he seems to focus exclusively on the individual with little room for social or systemic evil in his view of the world. The accents in preaching that he identifies are the goals of faith, life, church, family, hope, and prayer.[55] Correction of individual sin on its own cannot eliminate corporate sin that institutions commit (and humans in them) whatever the righteousness of its individuals. In Caemmerer, law is exclusively like a wagging finger of accusation and rebuke. His use of it to make people sorrowful, guilty, or anxious sounds manipulative today, however good his theological rationale may be. Some people might find his notion of gospel too unwaveringly christocentric, as though preachers cannot also be faithful at times preaching what Paul in Romans calls "the gospel of God."[56]

In recent times non-Lutherans have adopted, adapted, or extended law and gospel for homiletical purposes. In fact, sometimes it is the non-Lutherans, who have not been reared with these terms, who have seen in them the most preaching potential, perhaps because they are not battling old Lutheran arguments and negative associations.

HERMAN G. STUEMPFLE JR.

In 1978 two books appeared that radically changed the law/gospel territory for preaching. Herman G. Stuempfle Jr., at Lutheran Theological Seminary at Gettysburg, published *Preaching Law and Gospel,* while Milton Crum Jr., an Episcopalian at the Protestant Episcopal Theological Seminary in Virginia, wrote *Manual on Preaching: A New Process of Sermon Development.*

One might have expected Edmund A. Steimle, before either of them, to have written substantially on the subject. He taught at Union Seminary in New York City, where he taught several of the major homileticians of the present era, including Stuempfle. Steimle apparently spoke of law and gospel and approved of Farmer,[57] but there is little record of what he taught in this regard and no evidence that he conceived of them as more than ways to argue theologically.[58]

His student Herman Stuempfle, however, devised a more sophisticated understanding of law and gospel than had been plainly evident before by identifying two kinds of law and gospel. On the vertical access, the law functions as accusation and as a hammer of judgment that brings individuals to their knees in guilt and repentance. The corresponding kind of gospel is forgiveness. Historically, hammer of judgment and forgiveness tend to be the way in which law and gospel are portrayed in preaching. Stuempfle perceived a horizontal and descriptive dimension of them that he found in the Bible and Luther. Law is not just divine laws; it is a condition of human existence. Law as a "mirror of existence" reflects back to the world its fallen condition that includes anxiety, finitude, alienation, doubt, and despair.[59] A distinct kind of gospel is required to correlate with this. Stuempfle called it "gospel as antiphon to existence," that is, gospel that turns worldly expectations upside down.[60] He conceived of some biblical texts as wholly law or wholly gospel; yet "the actual sermon will not be without its counter dimension,"[61] for they are "the twofold form of the one Word and spoken by the one God."[62] The sermon may contain various alternatives: judgment and forgiveness, alienation and reconciliation, anxiety and certitude, despair and hope, or transience and homecoming,[63] all leading to a call to obedience.[64]

Stuempfle sounds like he is advocating a sequential movement of the sermon from law to gospel to obedience, because he called gospel an "antiphon"–a sounding back or overturning of something that has preceded it–and because obedience is a response to the gospel. However, he pulled back from advocating such a movement overall. Law and gospel are not sharp-boundaried components one may simply insert in a sermon (note in the following quotation the influence on him of Davis and organic form):

> [A] sermon is not a mechanism. It is a living entity whose genesis and growth are analogous to the wondrous process by which life is conceived and then develops in the womb. The sermon's creation cannot be programmed. It is not simply a total of interchangeable parts. The dimensions of Law, Gospel, and the call to obedience move within each sermon in lively, unpredictable ways. The form of each and the shape of the whole will be as unique in every event of proclamation as with each appearance of new life.[65]

Stuempfle consistently used the phrase "law and gospel." In so doing, he did more than point to the human impossibility of ever totally or appropriately separating law and gospel: A prescription "from law to gospel" is a "distortion."[66] His major accomplishment was providing freedom to preachers with his horizontal notions of law and gospel. Preachers uneasy about employing law from week to week lest they be mistaken for a critical parent had another way of fulfilling the responsibility to preach judgment. They could describe a situation of fallenness or brokenness in the world and society. Steumpfle found this a more congenial way of preaching in the post-Vietnam War era, though vertical law remained important. Moreover, he provided preachers with an understanding of gospel that emphasizes God's action to overturn the powers of this world. In a simple, brilliant, ninety-degree turn from vertical to horizontal, Steumpfle shifted the focus of preaching from being primarily individualistic to being social, as well. He still had not identified systemic dimensions of sin and evil in society, but he laid the foundation for others.[67]

MILTON CRUM

Milton Crum Jr.'s *Manual on Preaching* did not have much impact at the time of its publication, perhaps because of its complexity. However, directly and perhaps even coincidentally, it had enormous significance for homiletics as a whole. Crum was as convinced as homileticians before him that preaching was an event. Like an increasing number of them, he saw sermon structure in terms of movement. For him the sermon starts in an area of life that needs transformation by the gospel and moves to a place where that transformation makes a significant difference. Craddock had already started to mine the preacher's experience of the biblical text through the week as a source for sermon form and content.[68] Crum staked a claim in the same territory. He saw direct and immediate parallels among three elements: the preacher's hermeneutical process, "the overall plot of the biblical story," and the structure of sermon design.[69] In his mind, each of these three moves from *Situation* to *Complication* to *Resolution.*[70]

Crum devised five "dynamic factors" that ensure movement and "story-like structure":

1. symptomatic behavior
2. root
3. resulting consequences
4. gospel content
5. new results[71]

Combined with Situation, Complication, and Resolution, these dynamic factors work something like this: The Situation is the human situation "mucked up with sin" after the fall.[72] The Complication is what people experience as symptoms of their fallen attitudes, beliefs, or worldviews. This *symptomatic behavior* needs transformation by the gospel. The *root* of the behavior needs to be identified along with the *resulting consequences* to help people understand why they behave in certain ways. Crum could have used the term *analysis* to describe Complication.

Crum framed this in biblical and theological terms, not psychological. "This [root] is the area of the inner person: the mind which needs renewing (Romans 12:2), the heart which needs to be filled with good treasure (Luke 6:45), and the old nature which needs to be replaced by a new one (Ephesians 4:22–24)."[73] The Resolution is the *gospel content* that "speaks to the root of behavior to effect a transformation in mind and heart."[74] The preacher points to *new results* that follow the new way of perceiving or believing, including "new symptomatic behavior on the feeling and/or action levels and *new consequences* which follow as obedience to faith."[75]

Crum tried to keep the sermon process very fluid and struggled to find a way to avoid being mechanical; but in trying to accomplish this, his whole process drags to a halt. He speaks of four related components of the sermon that may be engaged in any order: biblical situation-complication, present situation-complication, biblical gospel resolution, and present gospel resolution.[76] In the end his dynamic process succumbs to a malaise that affects too many books in homiletics that are based in excellent ideas. It becomes too complicated and unwieldy. Bewildered students are left standing by the sermon roadside uncertain whether to walk, hitch a ride, or borrow a car.

Crum can be criticized for other things. For instance his discussion of "the overall plot of the biblical story" as Situation, Complication, Resolution, is too brief. Does he mean (1) that Bible stories often move like this or (2) that stories in general, including the Bible, tend move like this (as Aristotle noted), or (3) that biblical stories should be retold in this manner regardless of their plot? He could not mean that all biblical stories move like this or even that all biblical passages are stories. Perhaps the strongest objection can be made to his turning of law and gospel into what sounds like problem and solution. The gospel is never just a solution to a problem; it is a relationship with God. What solutions one may find to problems are the fruit of that lived relationship of faith, not a substitute for it.

Nonetheless, Crum is a key transitional figure in the law/gospel school of homiletical thought. He understood that law (he preferred the word *judgment*) and gospel are not just theological terms. They are hermeneutical lenses with which to view biblical texts. They are homiletical tools with which to structure sermons. Crum also had a free-flowing organic notion of structure. He emphasized that sermons are not just ideas addressed to minds. They also address behaviors, feelings, and perceptions. In the next chapter we will see how his influence spread and how others utilized and extended his insights. Prior to Crum, homileticians primarily considered law *and* gospel as repeated emphases within a sermon. Crum led the way to the later development of the law/gospel school, which picks up on H. Grady Davis and stresses *from* law *to* gospel. Here we will shift to the terms "trouble" and "grace." One major reason for doing this is to get away from the troublesome associations of law with Old Testament and gospel with New.

6

THEOLOGICAL STRUCTURE II

From Trouble to Grace

Milton Crum[1] anticipated several key developments in the law/ gospel school. Most significantly he proposed that the overall movement of the sermon be from law to gospel, or what we will call from trouble to grace. Over the next two decades, Crum would influence or anticipate the work of Eugene Lowry, Richard Lischer, and myself. I do not identify these connections to elevate Crum or to make his work (or ours) more significant than it is. I do not mean to ignore the fact that Crum was himself influenced by some people whom we have discussed and by others not identified here (e.g., the plot structure complication-resolution, for example, is in Robert Scholes and Robert Kellogg[2]). Tracing Crum's significance is a way of quickly reviewing developments to the present day, and also of indicating how subtle influences in homiletics (and other disciplines) often are.

Eugene Lowry and the Homiletical Plot

Eugene Lowry is a Methodist who has made an enormous contribution to law/gospel. His *The Homiletical Plot: The Sermon as Narrative Art Form,* published in 1980, met with huge response because, in less than one hundred pages, he made sense of the narrative movement by offering simple step-by-step directions to the preacher.

Lowry said he had been instructed in the school of "engineering forms" of sermons (what we are calling mechanical), sermons that had parts that were meant to fit together and seldom did. Davis, Craddock, Steimle, Niedenthal, Rice, and others were already speaking about story sermons. Lowry looked for an element common to story that could provide a new image for the preaching task. He found it in the idea that sermons need plot. Frederick Buechner, the Presbyterian minister and novelist, had already cast preaching in terms of drama in his now classic essay on preaching, *Telling the Truth, The Gospel as Tragedy, Comedy and Fairy Tale.* Buechner cast his vote for an order of progression: "The gospel is bad news before it is good news."[3] For him the tragedy is our sin; the comedy is that we are loved anyway; and the fairy tale is that extraordinary things happen by God's grace.[4] The plot Lowry came up with is a law/gospel plot that sounds like Buechner and Crum clarified and simplified to basic sequenced essentials.

Lowry and Crum

The parallels between Crum and Lowry suggest Lowry's dependence on him. Crum began with the *Situation* of human sin after the fall. Lowry begins with *upsetting the equilibrium* that awakens the congregation to their deeper anxiety or ambiguity[5] –something is not right. Crum's second step, *Complication,* points to the symptoms people experience in their own behavior, their fallen attitudes, beliefs, or worldviews. Lowry's second step is *analyzing the discrepancy* that he says moves "from specific behavior to underlying causes."[6] Crum's next steps are *resolution* and *gospel content* that address the root cause to effect a transformation in the mind and heart of the hearer. Lowry's third step is reversal and *disclosing the key to resolution.*[7] His fourth step is *experiencing the gospel.* Crum then moves to *new results* and "*new*

Milton Crum (1978) (*italics* his "Dynamic Factors")	Eugene Lowry (1980)
1. Situation	1. Upsetting the Equilibrium
2. Complication: *symptom, root, resulting consequences* (i.e., analysis)	2. Analyzing the Discrepancy
3. Resolution:	3. Disclosing the Key to Resolution
(a) *Gospel content*	4. Experiencing the Gospel
(b) *New Results:* "*new consequences* that follow"	5. Anticipating the Consequences

consequences that follow"[8] the new way of perceiving or believing, whereas Lowry moves to *anticipating the consequences.*

The Plot as a Loop

Lowry's clarity of vision is seen in his notion of plot as a kind of loop, like the *icthus* fish symbol turned on its nose. The sermon plot proceeds down until it reaches a place of reversal at which point the good news is disclosed. Then the movement ascends towards a climax. As with Crum, the gospel for Lowry is an event, an experience, as opposed to the reception of ideas. A further gift comes with his identification of the midway point as a reversal, which he defines as "turning things upside down."[9] This implies a spiritual transformation and provides visual reinforcement for preachers that a different kind of activity is engaged in in the second half of the sermon. He compares the reversal to "the action of pulling the rug out from under someone. Often it is necessary to *lay* the rug before one pulls."[10]

Lowry Revised

Lowry recently revised his plot by reducing his former five "sequencing strategies" to four in one loop:

1. conflict
2. complication
3. sudden shift
4. unfolding

The strategy formerly designated as "experiencing the gospel" may happen anywhere from the second to fourth stages, but he recommends, "about three-fourths into the sermon. Perhaps five-sixths is better. On rare occasions it may happen on the last line."[11] He wants preachers to "refuse to announce a conclusion in advance [and] 'keep the cat in the bag.'"[12] Ideally for him, preaching evokes the proclamation[13] and is not an exercise in cognitive instruction. Preaching makes tentative claims, hence his title, *The Sermon: Dancing the Edge of Mystery.* "Particularly when dealing with the 'ineffable,' the church is called toward the eloquence of the provisional. Such speech declares the truth, all the while knowing the truth cannot be uttered."[14]

A Critique of Lowry

This is one of those typical situations in homiletics in which the author perhaps needed to provide actual sermon examples to test his claims. A delay in introducing the gospel until the end of the sermon seems less than desirable, for when God suddenly comes into focus at the end of a sermon the gospel is not brought home and applied to the listener's life or the world. Considerable sermon time is needed to make the gospel concrete and to allow people to experience what God is accomplishing in and through them and others. Richard Eslinger defends Lowry, saying that a delay of grace to the final sixth of a sermon can be effective if it is vividly stated and experienced.[15] Alternatively, it may be that Lowry wants to avoid concretion of the gospel in the hope that it will be evoked from the listeners themselves, since that is his theme.

Richard Lischer and Sermon Direction

Richard Lischer, a Lutheran, published *A Theology of Preaching* in 1981 with revised editions appearing in 1992 and 2001.[16] An important chapter on law and gospel represents one of Lischer's key homiletical accomplishments in this work. A second is his fixing of the movement of law to gospel as a viable overall paradigm for preaching. Lischer followed the hints of this paradigm in Davis and Buechner and the first substantial claim to it in Crum.

Lischer and Crum

Once again we see the significant influence of Crum. He described the structure of sermon movement as: "Sermons, like the biblical story, will move from fallen humanity to redeemed humanity, from sin to faith, from darkness to light, from what Paul calls living 'according to the flesh' to living 'according to the spirit,' from condemnation to justification, from alienation to sanctification."[17]

Lischer discusses the movement of the sermon in similar ways. For him a sermon moves from "the primal unity in God" through "one or more of the following sets of antitheses: chaos to order, bondage to deliverance, rebellion to vindication, despair to hope, guilt to justification, debt to forgiveness, separation to reconciliation, wrath to love, judgment to righteousness, defeat to victory, death to life."[18] As he says, the "first word in each pairing is reported as 'bad news' for humanity."[19]

Lischer follows Crum and Stuempfle in allowing the law to function in a descriptive or horizontal manner, not just an accusatory vertical manner. Lischer also clarifies how gospel functions within the Old Testament. In so doing he distances himself from those who would preach law from the Old Testament and then switch to the New Testament for grace: "The Old Testament's antiphon to judgment is the gospel of: the covenant, the new covenant, deliverance from

Egypt, God's love for the lowly, the messianic promise, return from exile, the reign of God, the Day of the Lord."[20]

The Relationship of Law and Gospel

Lischer compares the relationship of law and gospel to two tones that are sounded together: "It is like listening to a bassoon and a flute playing the same note."[21] Still, several dangers need to be avoided in preaching law and gospel. These dangers include:

1. moralism that prescribes virtues as the means of apprehending God's grace rather than presenting them as goals or consequences of the gospel,[22]

2. preaching about the gospel, which he compares to "speaking about food to a starving person,"[23] instead of offering the benefits of Christ.

Law/Gospel as Deep Structure

As in Stuempfle, gospel for Lischer ends in obedience. He is not too concerned what terms people use for law-gospel-obedience. He offers "the three movements of the sermon": analysis, transition, and integration[24] (an apparent variation on Crum's Situation, Complication, Resolution). The realities they represent are basic to the preaching task. He wrote, "it is essential that the reader understand that what we are considering here are *not* design motifs, as though we were advocating a return to the predictable three-points-and-a-poem of yesteryear. Rather those are *theological* movements which continue to appear in sermons of every shape and design."[25] In other words, he identified the law/gospel movement as a kind of deep structure or grammar that can operate in sermons whatever the design. However, because law/gospel can be conceived as a form, Lischer's point is universally overlooked in homiletical literature. Typically the law/gospel movement is overlooked as a subform of many other forms that functions to produce hope.

Paul Wilson and the Sermon's Four Pages

Crum also anticipated some of my own work. My background is the United Church of Canada, a 1925 union of Methodist, Presbyterian, and Congregational denominations. I wrote at length about law and gospel in 1988,[26] seeing it as one of several tensions that produced a "spark" of imagination in a sermon. In a high school physics class we had had an old hand-cranked telephone generator. When the positive and negative wires were held too far apart or were touching, no spark was visible. However, a spark became plainly visible if the wires were close enough to have some relationship, whether the gap was the tiniest separation to several inches.

The Tension that Sparks Metaphor

Similar to what we saw with the two wires of the generator, S. T. Coleridge theorized that imagination functions in language by bringing two images or ideas into relationship. The tension or energy generated between the poles produces a third identity (or spark). The result is not a compromise of the sort that may happen with thesis-antithesis-synthesis in logic. The result is also not the actual reconciliation of opposites that I. A. Richards conceived when interpreting Coleridge, that is, two identities collapsing into one.[27] Rather, the result Coleridge intended is metaphor, a language event or tensive relationship in which the reader must participate to gain understanding. Each pole retains its own identity. The reader is drawn into a process of deconstruction (the metaphor not true, e.g., Jesus is not a vine) and of construction (the metaphor is true) that yields meanings. Law and gospel function in a sermon as two poles of a metaphor. The one says you are condemned and the other says you are saved. Both claims are true: We are sinners, and we are saved. The two are reconciled only in faith. In the tension between the two a new meaning emerges that is characterized by a relationship of trust and dependence upon Jesus Christ. We do as Paul instructed, we work out our salvation in fear and trembling (Phil. 2:12).

Conceiving of law and gospel in a tensive relationship that evokes a new identity in faith is a significant development. Most of the earlier work conceived of law and gospel in modernist ways: They were static alternatives to be applied mechanically to different kinds of people to produce contrast and comparison. The identities of law and gospel were separate and distinct, so preachers studying them focused on the individuality and independence of each, not on their interdependence and relationship. Preachers now focus on the way they affect each other, on the unity of the theological system they produce, on the flow from one to the other.

In illustration of this shift, when my *Imagination of the Heart: New Understandings in Preaching* went to press in 1988, the publisher's artist produced a book cover that utterly failed; it featured a heart. The design was too literal and lacked imagination. When the tensive relationship of two things producing a third was explained, the artist immediately thought of color. He then produced a cover that effectively demonstrated the book's content: a band of blue across the top, a band of yellow across the bottom, and a band of green across the middle, representing their union (yellow + blue = green). As part of this third identity an illusion of the whole was generated of sand, trees, and sky.

By coincidence, Walthers instructed his students to separate law and gospel, and not mix them, and he used the same analogy of yellow and blue: "Or look at the colors. Mix yellow and blue together, and you get neither blue nor yellow but green. And if in a sermon Law and Gospel are mingled, you get a third something that does not belong there."[28] Walthers conceived of law and gospel as two kinds of content that represent static entities like building blocks. He did not sense language having an organic and generative life of its own. His notion of law and gospel was linear, not tensive; literal, not metaphorical; mechanical, not organic; modern, not postmodern.

Postmodern Law and Gospel

A postmodern understanding conceives of law and gospel as two functions of theological language that generate and produce a desired outcome of preaching. Words are not chunks of preformed thought. Rather, language is what permits and generates thought. Thus in the juxtaposition between law and gospel, a linguistic tension, dynamic energy, current, or spark is created. This tensive spark helps to propel the sermon in a movement that traces the overall movement of the faith from expulsion from Eden to the New Jerusalem, from the exodus to the promised land, from the crucifixion to the resurrection, from Good Friday to Easter. Thus the sermon begins to tell the Christian story even in its structure and flow, with the help of the Holy Spirit. Theology gives direction to sermon form, and the sermon form shapes theological content.

At the same time, law and gospel must continually be reconceived, their tension sought anew; for gospel, once it is spoken into the world, easily deconstructs and becomes a new law in human hands. When this happens, we must again turn to the cross and empty tomb to find there the One who is both the fulfillment of the law and the good news for all time. Christ calls us back from our ministries to be renewed as his body and to receive the disruptive newness and power of the gospel. The gospel is necessarily given anew each moment; it is not something that flows automatically from the nature of God or is to be presumed by anyone. It derives from a relationship, and each offering is a specific act of self-giving grace that again conforms to the unique and decisive act that was accomplished once and for all on the cross. The tension between

Good Friday and Easter may be found in any moment. What distinguishes this polarity from typical modernist polarities (good-bad, right–wrong) is the dramatic movement forward that is provided by Christ's initiative in countering the law of death with the gift of his life. The new identity that is produced out of this tension is a dynamic relationship of faith and acceptance of unconditional love.

Trouble and Grace as Homiletical Tools

A further feature made law and gospel more accessible as homiletical tools. They can be confusing concepts for students to grasp at a practical level. Eugene Lowry, in a piano presentation to the Academy of Homiletics meeting in 1992, had spoken of the sermon as being like jazz, starting with trouble. Trouble seemed to me like a good word to replace law. The simplest way of separating trouble and grace out is to use these as working definitions: Trouble puts the burden on humanity to act; grace puts the burden on God, and God has already accepted that burden in Jesus Christ. If the emphasis is on humanity to act, the notion is primarily trouble; if the emphasis is on God's empowering action, the notion is primarily grace.

A biblical text can be broken down into many concerns of the text. These are complete short sentences that focus on one idea in a text. Each short sentence focuses on a different idea; thus every text can produce a plentiful supply of options. They represent contact points between the text and today when they are transposed into concerns of the sermon. These transposed concerns, by contrast, have to do with now and use contemporary idiom. They vary from concerns of the text in one or two words that indicate the shift of time to the present. For example, in 1 Kings 17, a concern of the text might be: The widow's son was dead. Its transposed concern of the sermon might be: Many of us are dead. (This idea obviously needs sermonic clarification and expansion.) I encourage students as part of their exegetical process to follow certain steps:

1. Break down biblical texts into as many concerns of the text as possible.
2. Divide these into potential trouble concerns, grace concerns, and theologically neutral concerns.
3. Transpose the strongest ones into concerns of the sermon.
4. Choose the strongest grace pairing to be the MCT/MCS as the focus for the sermon.

Every sermon employs trouble and grace concerns whether the preacher is aware of these categories or not. Most preachers simply do not know how to take advantage of them and harness their energy and theological insight for preaching.[29]

The Hermeneutical Spiral

Several of these trouble and grace paired units (a concern of the text and a concern of the sermon) might be used in a sermon. While I like Lowry's loop, I needed to adapt it, for he had not discussed the biblical text or how the dialogue between the biblical text and our time fit into his "plot." I chose the image of a hermeneutical spiral, or a circle that spirals: it still had the overall downward and upward movement, but it added mini-loops. Each mini-loop signified the biblical text (down) and our situation (up).

God and the Theme Sentence

Two topics became particularly important for me in *Imagination of the Heart.* One had to do with the theme sentence. Unless the theme sentence itself focuses on God, God is not likely to have significant focus in the sermon. Said another way, unless the focus is on God, gospel cannot be gospel. Of course, a text may lean towards humanity, and some people may think that my God-centered approach fits all texts into a predetermined mold. Even if this were true, we are called to preach the gospel, not a text or what we define as a text. Texts are essential instruments that assist us. Having the Bible in the sermon is no guarantee that it possesses the gospel, but some texts are too narrow. Our approach encourages the sermon to focus both on what the text says about humanity and on what it says and implies about God. Unless the focus of the theme sentence is on God's action, gospel in the sermon will be an abstract idea; and unless the focus is an action of grace, the good news will be cast as judgment.

The Gospel and Social Justice Issues

The second essential learning came from Herman G. Stuempfle's understanding of horizontal law and gospel, because this opened the door to preaching on issues of social justice (the subject of upcoming chapters). Vertical notions of law and gospel cast God up above and us down below, as before a judge: We are found guilty even as God in Christ intercedes and forgives us. Horizontal law and gospel are easier to hear in our day. A mirror is held up to us so that we can see the world in all of its fallen condition, and we are awakened to the needs of others. The gospel comes as God's action that overturns the powers of death, injustice, and greed.

Part of the reason this is so liberating for preachers is that they do not have to wag a finger at the congregation in order to preach law effectively. Both kinds of law have their place. With horizontal law the stance of the preacher is not condemnation for doing wrong but empathy, helping listeners to understand why it is that we do what we do. For example, instead of only condemning racial intolerance, a preacher might help people to understand that it is spawned by fear of difference, a fear that has already been overcome in Christ's death and resurrection. Instead of condemning someone for taking drugs, a preacher could help listeners understand that the urge for drugs is akin to the need for meaning in life, but the need is simply being met in the wrong ways. Instead of going to God, we may turn to seemingly more immediate gratification. Empathy is key. The gospel in such a case is to be derived from the biblical text at hand, but it might have something to do not only with God's love, but also with God's delight in empowering change and in bringing all of God's children home. In other words, gospel need not be restricted in preaching to forgiveness or the individual's right relationship with God, for it also extends to God's willingness to get involved in human affairs.

Simplifying the Process

In *The Practice of Preaching* (1995),[30] I expanded concerns of the text to include sources beyond the text itself, including language study, archeology, history, geography, sociology, theology, commentaries, and so forth. Loops can be a helpful way of picturing the interchange of Bible and the current situation, but each loop need not begin with a textual insight. Sermons often contain many loops of varying sizes, but too many loops can be confusing for hearers as well as for the budding preacher. Multiple loops now seemed unnecessarily cumbersome. The sermon could end up sounding like popcorn being made—every few seconds there is a new focus.

Thus in *The Four Pages of the Sermon: A Guide to Biblical Preaching* (1999), I simplified the instructional process to one loop for trouble and one for grace (though in practice a sermon may still have many— as many as the number of times the preacher dips into the text).[31] For purposes of sermon unity, I encouraged preachers to select the major concern of the text first and then determine its inverse or flip side. This flip side focuses on the sin or brokenness in the biblical text that was the occasion for God's action. By thus inverting the major concern, a preacher may determine the trouble (i.e., a concern of the text and the concern of the sermon that will provide the trouble focus for the first half). Judgment and grace thus fit hand and glove. Trouble concerns can be found in texts that are predominantly grace, and grace concerns can be found in texts that are predominantly law or command. Stephen Farris has shown both in his paper, "Preaching Law as Gospel"[32] and in his new preaching commentary on texts of grace.[33]

The sermonic process was further simplified. To ensure sermon unity I recommended a sermon checklist: one text, one theme, one doctrine, one need (that is met in someone's life), one image, one mission (i.e., one desired outcome of a sermon). The image of a spiral was exchanged for the image of four pages of a sermon; what this image lacked in elegance, it gained in visual and practical value. Preachers could imagine a page as a metaphor for one quarter of a sermon. Page One was Trouble in the Biblical Text; Page Two was Trouble in Our World; Page Three was Grace in the Biblical Text; and Page Four was Grace in Our World. One can shuffle the pages to rearrange the sermon though grace is almost always the end note.

In this last move, Crum had already pointed the way, although I have seen it only recently. As noted above, his proposal ultimately collapsed under the weight of too many variables. Even the chart he provided as a schema of his hermeneutical process only confused issues, not least because it contained eight boxes with arrows going in every direction.[34] Still, if one could stay on the journey with him, he was clear when he said: "we are trying to articulate and examine a hermeneutical process, whose structure not only parallels the structure of sermon design but also the structure of the overall plot of the biblical story."[35]

Crum took readers through components of the sermon that included, in any order, biblical situation-complication, present situation-complication, biblical gospel resolution, and present gospel resolution. This sounds like four pages in embryonic form, with trouble in the first two and grace in the last two, though he never developed it or argued any priority of sequence: "The order of thought process in practice may correspond to the order of our description, or it may be quite different."[36]

Assessment

The Critiques of Trouble/Grace

We have traced the evolution of the trouble/grace school with such care because the subject is a dominant theological theme in homiletical literature. Trouble/grace may be viewed in many ways, but it is not often recognized as a school. Rather, it is stereotypically apprized as one sermon method among many. Typically it is compared alongside doctrinal, thematic, expository, Puritan plain style, three point, imagistic, moves and structures, text-shaped, narrative centered, or narrative plot sermons.[37] Alternatively it is seen as Lutheran. Sometimes it is equated with "an evangelistic sin-to-salvation paradigm, or a therapeutic brokenness to wholeness model."[38] Or it is interpreted as a way of circumscribing biblical texts with one particular method. It is sometimes dismissed as a problem/solution model, failing to recognize that gospel is relationship. Finally, it may be recognized as an approach that this or that individual homiletician might follow, but it is not recognized as a movement or school, and certainly not as a school of deep homiletical structure or grammar as opposed to surface structure.

Trouble/Grace as Deep Grammar

The trouble/grace school seeks to devise a way to ensure that both the divine and human dimensions of texts are identified. Such assessments as those above not only reduce the trouble/grace paradigm to one sermon model, they also fail to acknowledge the difference between anthropocentric sermons and those that center on God. Trouble/grace can be a model, but more precisely it can support many models and can serve as a deep grammar of them all. It claims that preaching is primarily a biblical and theological task and offers a teachable means that actually helps preachers to do good theology.

The trouble/grace school has devised numerous tools to assist preachers. Some are hermeneutical. Trouble and grace are set up as two theological lenses with which to view texts. The principle of theological inversion allows one to discover in a text what is present but not immediately obvious. Some tools are more purely theological. Trouble and grace are seen as dynamics within the same unified Word. While both make truth claims, neither one erases the other. In faith grace always proves stronger. Some tools are homiletical. Moving *from* trouble *to* grace in a sermon helps ensure that grace is stronger and reinforces the overall movement of the faith: *from* the exodus *to* the promised land, *from* the crucifixion *to* the resurrection and glory.

Further, trouble and grace complement each other in the sermon: the appropriate kind of trouble (vertical or horizontal) is met by the appropriate kind of grace (either forgiveness [vertical] or God overcoming the powers of death [horizontal]). Trouble and grace determine how Christ is portrayed in a sermon, whether as example and model (= law) or as Savior (=grace). Moreover, within homiletics, terms like trouble and grace, focus and function statements, concerns of the text and concerns of the sermon, major concerns, moves, loop and loops, reversal, pages, and the like help students to organize their material, structure their sermons, and discover what can be said about something from a theological perspective. With such tools, sermons from history can be read with some degree of critical awareness (beyond saying they seem boring). Finally, in harnessing the tension of trouble and grace within a sermon, students learn something about how metaphor functions, not only because metaphor is essential to do theology, but also because the trouble/grace dynamic in itself is metaphor writ large. By juxtaposing trouble and grace, and by the power of the Holy Spirit, a third identity is generated, an identity of faith, hope, and love of God and neighbor. The result is far from a static modern notion of polar opposites; it is a generative postmodern tension that momentarily resists deconstructive tendencies in favor of a strong claim on behalf of God.

The Goal of Sermons

Within the trouble/grace school a certain degree of consensus has developed concerning sermons. Sermons should have certain characteristics:

1. be hopeful
2. build up the community of faith
3. present the biblical text as the sermon's source
4. identify what needs correction in human behavior
5. portray human experience in authentic ways
6. draw on the rich resources of language, ideas, images, and stories
7. guide people to deeper theological awareness of the trouble
8. bring theological reflection to bear on the world
9. cast people on God's gracious resources for help
10. demonstrate God's action in human affairs
11. speak of God in concrete ways as a Person (as one in three Persons)
12. represent tradition faithfully
13. proclaim what God has done and is doing
14. permit God to speak in present tense unconditional declaration
15. empower individuals to greater faith
16. equip individuals for lives of faithful service to others

17. encourage people to use the gifts God has given them
18. promise the resources they will continue to find in God
19. point to what God is already doing to change the world
20. allow the beginning and the end of time to inform the current time
21. attend to signs of trouble and grace as signatures of God
22. seek echoes of trouble and grace throughout the Bible
23. uncover trouble and grace in or behind each biblical text
24. preach the gospel, not just the biblical text
25. celebrate the good news

Discussion Starters for Evaluating Trouble/Grace

These are just some of the assumptions in the current literature. Whatever the reasons that little discussion of the trouble/grace school in homiletics has occurred, the purpose of identifying it now is to facilitate such discussion, to establish better the discipline of homiletics academically, to help negotiate its directions, and to improve the teaching of preaching. Such discussion directed at trouble/grace will ask crucial questions such as: Ought sermons be hopeful even if a text (or a preacher) is not? Are texts legitimately to be read from the perspectives of trouble and grace? Does law to gospel restrict and reshape a biblical text, or does it honor it? Ought preaching a text to be compatible with preaching the gospel? What notions of text are best upheld in preaching? Are there other ways sermons legitimately produce hope? What is the role of theology in reading texts?

Such discussion will help homiletics move to new ways of rendering scripture and God. As a discipline, homiletics has made little progress in identifying excellence, and to the degree that preaching is a theological task, the identification of excellence will have something to do with theological structure and theological guidelines for the sermon. Homiletics is already starting to do a much better job than it has on the important subject of ethics, to which we will return in the next section. A key question will be: Is preaching grace compatible with preaching ethics? Before we get to that, we now turn to explore what alternatives there are to the trouble/grace theology of preaching.

7

VARIATIONS AND ALTERNATIVE THEOLOGIES OF PREACHING

The trouble/grace school of homiletics is perhaps the only one that is explicitly theological. For its structural guidelines it looks to a theological purpose of preaching, to preach the gospel and build a community of hope. However, the trouble/grace school owns no monopoly on theological options in homiletics. Other positions homileticians have taken concerning theology of the Word have implications for structure, and we will examine six. Three of these are independent variations on trouble/grace–by which I mean they did not arise out of direct dialogue with it. I will argue that they belong as a huge part of it: Bryan Chapell comes from an evangelical perspective, while Mary Catherine Hilkert writes from the Roman Catholic perspective. I also include much of what is known today as African American preaching, recognizing the inadequacy of this term as a catchall for many traditions that have many variations. Three other scholars provide quite distinct theologies with structural implications, two seemingly rooted in event and one opposed to event: Presbyterian Charles Bartow, United Methodist Marjorie Hewitt Suchocki, and Presbyterian Charles Campbell.

Variations on Trouble/Grace

Bryan Chapell: Preaching as Redemptive Theology

Bryan Chapell, homiletics professor and dean of faculty at Covenant Theological Seminary, wants to restore Christ-centered expository preaching. For him, "all of God's Word [is] a unified message of human need and divine provision."[1] He has preachers determine first what is the Fallen Condition Focus (FCF) of a biblical text that points to human sinfulness, our fallen condition, or the world's brokenness (he does not use the word *law*). "A message that merely establishes 'God is good' is not a sermon. However, when the same discourse deals with the doubt we may have that God is good when we face trial and demonstrates from the text how we handle our doubt with the truth of God's goodness, then the preacher has a sermon."[2]

A Lived Response to Grace

For Chapell the sermon is based on a proposition, yet the goal of the sermon is no longer just information. The goal is the listener's lived response to God's grace in text-directed ways. Designed with this in mind, sermon "messages will not simply tell people to hunker down and try harder this week, but will lead them to understand that Christ's work rather than their own provides the only hope of Christian obedience."[3] Chapell adds, "when people walk away from a message understanding that grace both motivates and enables them to serve God, futile human striving and vain self-vaunting vanish."[4] However broken or sinful we are in our fallen condition, God's redemptive work in Jesus Christ is of larger, ultimate significance that needs loud heralding in the sermon. Chapell admits that such a principle may "seem to stretch the bounds of precise expository preaching."[5]

How can the preacher remain Christ-centered when thousands of passages are Christ-silent? Chapell's solution is to "place every text within a redemptive context."[6] Do not impose Jesus on the text, but rather discern "the place and role of the text in the entire revelation of God's redemptive plan."[7] Sermons become christocentric not by citing the name of Jesus, but by demonstrating "the reality of the human predicament that requires divine solution."[8] Every biblical text, Chapell says, is predictive of, preparatory for, reflective of, and/ or resultant of the work of Christ. To those who wonder about whether his hermeneutical approach is justified, Chapell responds with his view of scripture: "Why does all Scripture focus on some aspect of our fallen condition? The clear answer is: to supply the warrant and to define the character of the redemptive elements in Scripture that we can, in turn, apply to our fallenness. The Bible's ultimate aim is beautifully positive. Scripture addresses features of our incompleteness only because such a focus concurrently signals the work of God that makes us whole."[9]

CHALLENGES TO CHAPELL

One can challenge Chapell. For instance, is preaching primarily an event of encounter with God, or with God's message, or with God's redemptive work as Chapell maintains? Listeners can encounter God's redeeming work without encountering God in the same way that people can encounter nature without meeting the Creator. The difference may be in whether God is simply assumed by the preacher and listener to be present in and through the sermon (with all that that means both in terms of the sermon as God's act and in terms of a listener's attitude and state of receptivity) or whether God's presence is actively identified and proclaimed.

Another question arises: Is it possible to move into a biblical text only once in a sermon (as his explanation-illustration-application format implies) and to emerge having given sufficient biblical or theological attention to both trouble and grace? In all likelihood one or the other will receive emphasis, or both will be presented in a back and forth fashion that allows neither to be heard clearly and the effect is to cancel each other. Clearly his focus is on the redemptive work of God in Jesus Christ, and his scholarly influences are not in the tradition of Luther or Barth; yet he has been led to an approach that closely resembles law and gospel. His work helpfully informs it, for instance in his fallen condition focus and in his positive view of the role and purpose of scripture. Chapell also understands that homiletical method is a theological issue, not merely a question of form or function considered separate from the Word we are seeking to proclaim or the faith we are seeking to foster.

Mary Catherine Hilkert: Preaching as Sacramental Imagination

Mary Catherine Hilkert, associate professor of theology at the University of Notre Dame and a Dominican (The Order of Preachers), is on an ecumenical search for a more adequate understanding of the preaching event. She wants preaching to be reconceived as naming grace. Protestant dialectical theology, for instance Barth, Bultmann, and Ebeling, fails to seek or discover revelation directly within human history or creation. Hilkert thinks that the dialectic between judgment and grace in Luther prevents grace from being viewed "as radical transformation of the human person or society."[10] The problem rests more specifically in Luther's characterization of the believer justified by faith but still at once righteous and sinning–*simil iustus et peccator.*

DIALECTICAL AND SACRAMENTAL

She wants preaching to retain from dialectical theology the word of judgment and from Roman Catholic sacramental theology the art of naming grace in the depths of human experience. She calls this an act of sacramental imagination. It is the art of "seeing the world through an alternative lens"; she sees this as the Catholic contribution to the ecumenical discussion of preaching. The starting place will not be defeat of the power of sin and death in the resurrection and the power of the proclaimed Word to transform sinful humanity. Rather preaching will be understood incarnationally and redemptively. God being found active in and through humanity effects a real inner transformation of the human person. Reflection on experience is needed not to make preaching relevant, but to hear God's Word today. Preaching will "point to the mystery of God at the heart of human existence." Preaching will not offer an interpretation of life but will invite people to "come and see" and "go and do likewise."[11]

LOCATING PREACHING IN LIBERATING COMMUNITIES

Such preaching can take place only within communities dedicated to liberation from oppression, to transforming lives with healing compassion and mercy. Salvation will be understood as a communal event, naming God's actions in the depths of the community's narrated human experience. Sacramental theology views experience and human words as potential sacraments of divine love. Thus signs of grace are everywhere for those who have eyes to see. Preaching awakens what is already present in the depths of a person by grace (Karl Rahner).[12] It involves pointing to God's presence in history and today (Edward Schillebeeckx).[13] For Hilkert, conversion of the heart cannot be separate from transformation of oppressive political, social, and ecclesial structures, not least those that deny women the office of preacher.

Hilkert has an important focus on social justice and on grace as radical transformation of society to conform to God's will. She says that most people's contemporary experience of God "is in the face of, and in spite of, human suffering."[14] In Roman Catholic theology, grace includes common grace rooted in creation that remains in spite of the fall. Hilkert emphasizes the goodness of creation both as a way to affirm the goodness of the human body and as a way of saying that not every situation is hopelessly corrupt and in need of healing. Her vision of sacramental imagination, while it is not a practical homiletic, reconfigures reality by seeing it from the perspective of grace and God's promise. Her vision attends to the reality of evil, violence, and human suffering. It affirms that the power of God's grace is stronger than the power of human sin. It emphasizes human responsibility to act.

The preacher points to the world and finds in human experience that which transcends it and names it as grace. The closest she gets to a homiletic may be her clever adaptation of Paul Ricoeur: "effective narrative preaching involves the threefold pattern of prefiguration of past human experience, configuration of the human story in light of the divine plot of the story of Jesus, and refiguration of imagination and life through the ongoing process of conversion."[15]

A CRITIQUE OF HILKERT

Apparently, Hilkert has not read broadly in Protestant homiletics for its notions of grace. She could have benefited in particular from Stuempfle's emphasis on naming grace in the vertical and horizontal modes and from Crum and those building on him in the structural design of the sermon with its attendant implications. Hilkert is in agreement with using grace as a lens with which to view the world and to identify God's action in individuals and in world events. Through preaching, the mystery of God's presence in the world becomes evident, and faith communities are formed. The world is seen in a new way, reconfigured by the gospel. Many people will resonate with her notion of looking in places of suffering to find God and of listening to the people name grace in those situations. Still, the preaching act in Hilkert's view seems to be less than an event of encounter with God and more like listening for an indirect word from God. She remains satisfied to hear the voice of a messenger who has seen God in the world rather than the voice of God. Does the Christ who is preached not also do the preaching?[16] Her account does not retain a tensive relationship between trouble and grace. In this, she removes from her theology the possibility of that tensive relationship providing structural guidance to sermons or to preachers seeking to improve their pastoral theological reflection.

African American Preaching: Preaching as Celebration and Experience

Both Chapell and Hilkert tend to diminish event and thus may lose God and what Gerhard Forde called present-tense unconditional declaration of good news from God.[17] What is known in homiletical literature as African American preaching by contrast maximizes event. Like Euro-American preaching it has much diversity within it. Several key books articulate perspectives on black preaching theory and advocate preaching that ends in celebration.

HENRY H. MITCHELL

Although Henry H. Mitchell's *Preaching as Celebration and Experience* claims connections with David Buttrick, its starting point is radically different. Manuals on pulpit oratory have long stressed Aristotle's idea: to *convince,* you address the *reason;* to *persuade,* you appeal to the *emotions.* With recent interest in narrative and emotion, most homiletical texts give primacy to the power of narrative to convince, to reach the mind through conscious or subconscious means, whether by deductive or inductive reasoning. There is no point traveling with Mitchell unless you are ready to address the importance of passion, "emotion," "intuition," "experience," or, as he frequently calls it, "celebration," in preaching. The sermon still produces cognitive purpose by the "controlling idea" (i.e., theme sentence) and by the need to "show" the truth of ideas. But the bottom line is an "affective purpose," synthesizing what he calls the "logic of emotive consciousness" and "the logic of human reason." The entire being of the preacher embodies the message to the whole person in the pew.

If we recognize that Mitchell is talking less about form than he is about affective performance, the seemingly familiar scenery begins to look different. In his discussion of narrative, for instance, the function of identity is not to bring home the truth of an idea so much as it is to celebrate what he calls "*ecstatic reinforcement* of the truth portrayed."[18] We remember our own best encounters with God, those holy moments in our lives that Mitchell says have been the best-kept secret of homiletics. People "*do* what they celebrate,"[19] which is one reason that the preacher must encourage the congregation to feel the contagious joy of what is preached. Celebration, he says, not exhortation, is the best way to motivate people.

Because of the emotive dimension of preaching, even the way Mitchell and others plot sermons cannot be conceived in strictly linear fashion. Samuel Proctor employs Hegel's thesis, antithesis, and synthesis as does James Harris; but it is linear logic with a transformative difference.[20] Mitchell speaks of narrative sermons involving "setting, plot-conflict, protagonist and cast, resolution, and celebration."[21] He speaks of the flow of the sermon in Buttrick's terms, as being "like acts of a play, which now are often referred to as 'moves'...[They] may look like the old outline of abstract points or general statements, but they are radically different. They are movements in consciousness made real by the supply of details crucial to the development of the plot."[22]

FRANK THOMAS

Sermons may admonish and discuss the sins, "don'ts and other negatives"; but the opening should not consist of these, and no more than a third of the entire sermon ought to be in this vein.[23] Frank Thomas's preaching worksheet echoes perhaps Crum as well as Wilson, "What is the 'bad news' in the text? What is the 'bad news' for our time?" and "What is the 'good news' in the text? What is the 'good news' for our time?"[24] Mitchell describes the movement of the sermon as "from analytical style and logical impressiveness to the flow and beauty of poetry."[25] Thomas describes sermon design in terms of emotion: "the sermonic design is an emotional process that culminates in a moment of celebration when the good news (the assurance of grace) intensifies in core belief until one has received an inner assurance, affirmation, courage, and a feeling of empowerment."[26]

From trouble to grace is thus a discernable movement. The driving force seems to be the impetus to celebrate what God has done, is doing, and is demonstrating in the Holy Spirit. Such action and demonstration occurs in both the preacher and the congregation at the climax of the sermon and through the service of worship.

CLEOPHUS LARUE

Cleophus LaRue says that people in his tradition gather in worship "to be assured and reassured that God has acted and will act for them and for their salvation."[27] As part of his initial formative approach to the biblical text, La Rue looks for the divine initiative in it. He seeks some area of congregational experience the text addresses,[28] and determines whether "God's power is used to liberate, deliver, provide, protect, empower, or transform."[29] The sermon he analyzes of Jeremiah Wright[30] seems to move much as Mitchell describes, with no more than thirty per cent given to trouble and the latter half of the sermon rising to celebration.

Trouble and grace as they appear in African American preaching arise out of centuries of oppression preceded by an even longer heritage of celebration in ancient African traditions. It does not arise initially out of contact with Luther and his writings. Thus if the preaching resonates with the trouble/grace school, it does so out of similar discovery that for people to be uplifted, the sermon needs to move to hope. There is no set form for varieties of black preaching (or any other kind). It has many forms, but we may note that African American preaching that draws on oral tradition never lost story while much other preaching has had to scramble to recover it. The move to celebration is a theological movement at a deep structural level that manifests itself in performance of the gospel. The fact that published African American sermons typically are long also may mean that within the sermon trouble and grace do not need to be so clearly delineated or separated as is important when sermons are compressed by time constraints and the flavor of each may be easily lost.

Alternatives to Trouble/Grace

Charles L. Bartow: Preaching as God's Human Speech

Charles L. Bartow has a lively conception of God's action in preaching for which he does use the actual word *event*, but more frequently refers to as "*actio divina,* God's self-performance."[31] God is totally free to use human words in any way God chooses to disclose divine reality. God is in no way bound by human ideas of who God should be. Some of these ways can be baffling, like scriptural oxymoron, metaphor, and metonymy concerning God. The words of scripture are not "seemingly human, docetic. Instead, they are really human through and through."[32] God uses them to God's purposes. Scriptural witness has more power to disclose any aspect of life than we ourselves might be able to discern, even with our best hermeneutical strategies and theories.

OBEDIENCE OF LIBERATION

In the proclamation of Christ we are fettered by God's Word and "captured" in an "obedience of liberation"[33] through which we are dead to sin. Thus in the *actio divina* are two emphases:

1. God's self-performance of who God is
2. God's recreation of humanity in divine likeness

God uses multiple (and in the eternal Word, limitless) experiences in this self-performance; thus this pluralism of experience is open to interpretations. However provisional these are, the revelation they bear is definitive and reliable.

In preaching, the *actio divina* and the *homo performans* encounter each other. Scriptural witness is narrated and interpreted with reference to the confessional and creedal traditions of the church, and something happens; "God takes us as we are and presses us into the service of what God would have us be."[34] Bartow wants sermons to be thought of like texts of scripture as "arrested performances." The sermon is

> a happening about to happen again. It is a world of meaning entangled in words waiting to be disentangled. It is blood turned into ink that, through speech, may be turned back into blood. It is not like milk bottled and ready to be delivered to market. From exegesis to speech to hearing–and to liturgical, ethical, and missional enactment–it is performance, form coming through. It is witness as event, as felt claim and succor.[35]

BARTOW'S GUIDELINES FOR PREACHING

How does all of this translate into practical homiletical advice? Bartow offers five guidelines for preachers:

1. Preaching has a *present tense tone.* (Texts are treated "as worlds of meaning evoked and engaged in living speech.")
2. Preaching emphasizes the *divine initiative.* (It reveals how in a text and in Christ, "God takes us as we are and presses us into the service of what God would have us be.")
3. Preaching offers a *Christian interpretation of life.* (It empowers congregants to critical and faithful theological reflection in line with scripture and tradition.)
4. Preaching is in the *indicative mood.* (It generates awareness of God's dialogic address of silence and speech, claim and succor.)
5. Preaching features a *dexterous use of a variety of sermon strategies, and its diction (word choice) aims at cause, not effect.* (Cause depicts scenes that stir up connotative responses, while effect identifies what those responses should be.)[36]

A CRITIQUE OF BARTOW

One strength of Bartow's offering is his theological use of performative language. He encourages preachers to bring their best gifts and resources to the human performance of preaching without diminishing divine freedom to do whatever God wants with our words in the *actio divina.* Two performances are going on: God is loving people as they are and enlisting them in service. Bartow's guidelines are fresh (for instance, his distinction between focusing on cause not effect) as is the attitudinal and cognitive perspective he offers on human and divine performance in preaching. Many of his ideas so resonate with the trouble/grace school, it would be good to hear him enter into dialogue with it to better assess the utility of his suggestions.

Marjorie Hewitt Suchocki: Preaching and the Whispered Word

Marjorie Hewitt Suchocki speaks of the whispered word not as a recommendation for a preaching voice but as a description, in process theology, of the manner in which God's ever-creative word encounters the individual. Without this word there can be no creaturely existence, for "the everlasting God is the everlasting Creator."[37] Nothing can exist without this word being constantly directed toward it. This word comes repeatedly as a call awaiting response, yet the initial coming of this word is at subconscious levels that only eventually are recognized consciously. God's word is always redemptive, transformative, and incremental. That is to say that God always knows the steps that we as humans need to take to get out of the messes we get into. God keeps proposing them to us in often hidden incarnational ways through small steps and often mundane events.

Four Justifications for Word as a Whispered Word

Suchocki offers four justifications for this word as a whispered word:

1. We may not recognize this word because it is so easily drowned out by events around us: "It is clothed in the past even as it bespeaks a future, and it leads us not through extraordinary leaps and bounds, but most often through a quite ordinary faithfulness in the midst of things."[38]

2. Since there is never a moment in which this word is not directed to us as humans, we might not even recognize God's word because, like our heartbeat, it is always there.

3. "By the time consciousness is achieved, the initial word has been transformed into a subjective word of one's own intent."[39] In other words, life is a becoming process, a process of becoming ourselves in each moment.

4. God's word is whispered by God's own design, such that our response is directed not back to God so much as forward and toward the world and communal good: "It's as if God creates

within the depths of each one of us, and also on the surface *through* each one of us."[40]

Suchocki concludes that God's word "is a whisper, almost out of the range of our hearing...almost."[41]

THE REVEALED AND PROCLAIMED WORD AS SUPPLEMENTS

In preaching, this hidden word of God is supplemented by the revealed word of God and the proclaimed Word. They have the potential to "intensify the whispered word, magnifying its creative power"[42] and raise it in our consciousness to the level of a shout.

Without preaching we have no access to God, yet through it God is made audibly and visually present to us. We are invited, judged, and empowered to create community in God's image, pleasing to God and contributing to the welfare of the earth. For Suchocki, the Trinitarian act of God of creating, redeeming, and unifying/sanctifying in the macrocosm is repeated in the microcosm through the whispered word that is the basis of our existence. Through preaching, the redemptive Word of the gospel and the creative word by which God calls us into being are unified as one Word by the work of the Spirit.[43] Preaching, she says, "in an identity-forming event."[44]

THEMES FOR PREACHING

At least as far back as the origin of systematic theology, preachers have been identifying great themes around which to preach the faith. Suchocki identifies seven:

1. the universe as the creation of God
2. the problem of sin
3. the provision of sin's answer in Jesus Christ who reveals God to us
4. the possibility of new life that triumphs over sin
5. the creation of community
6. the work of God through that community in the world
7. the hope of everlasting redemption[45]

She calls these symbols rather than doctrines because "symbols are deeper than doctrine or theology." For Suchocki, preaching theologically involves finding one of these "fundamental symbols"[46] in the biblical text at hand and letting it interact with one's denominational tradition. As a homiletical approach she recommends:

"Weave text and tradition together, or contrast the text with the tradition, or let the contrasts and/or conflicts within the text and the tradition push toward yet one more transformation of the symbol involved."[47] For instance, she points out that in John 9 the blindness of the man should not be taken as a symbol for sin (thereby doing a disservice to the text and those who are physically blind), for the man is able to see spiritually before his physical healing. Thus the text is against willful spiritual blindness.[48]

A CRITIQUE OF SUCHOCKI

Suchocki's understanding of the whispered word is appealing, not least as a description of how we often experience God's Word coming to us in often slowly dawning awareness and with incremental sanctifying grace. One could wish that the process of becoming ourselves that she outlines had more obvious biblical warrant and that it did not seem at times to sideline the Christ event. Her process theology paradigm, like Hilkert's sacramental imagination, yields a universe that is infused with grace. More homiletical safeguards need to be developed to uphold this insight and to avoid the danger of preaching nature and whatever one takes in nature to be God.

Charles L. Campbell: Preaching and Postliberal Theology

THEOLOGY OF HANS FREI

Charles L. Campbell is a Presbyterian who teaches at Columbia Theological Seminary. He finds in the theology of Hans Frei a perspective that takes issue with preaching as word-event, particularly as it manifests itself in the New Hermeneutic and narrative preaching.[49] Frei opposed liberal theology for its attempt to "correlate" the faith with human experience and to explain how the human condition makes faith meaningful. The focus of such theology is faith and anthropology, not God. Liberals assumed that human need and experience were universal and were determined independent of Christian beliefs and practices.[50] They focused on how Jesus Christ is present rather than on who he is. The goal of Frei's cultural-linguistic theology is dogmatics and the unsubstitutable identity of Jesus Christ,[51] not the inner experience of the individual as the standard of meaning.[52] Narrative helpfully provides "thick description," instead of explanation, and thus remains subordinate to the biblical story. The gospel stories have no external meaning apart from Jesus, who is their subject matter and "literal sense."[53] Frei is not concerned with the genre of narrative: Theology is narrative to the extent that it focuses descriptively on the content of the Bible story, on what Jesus did and underwent. The test is not explanation and whether Jesus makes sense of our experience, but whether we will follow him and allow faithful community to be formed by his identity.[54]

In the cultural-linguistic model of Frei (and George Lindbeck), religion does not give expression to a universal human experience. Rather religion functions as a kind of culture and language that shapes religious experience in distinct ways. In fact, religion makes religious experience possible. All of this apparently puts Campbell (and Frei) at odds with much contemporary event-centered homiletics that employs an "experiential-expressivist" model: "This 'Word-event'...is understood primarily in experiential terms; the sermon becomes an 'experiential event' in which transformation is supposed to happen experientially in individuals."[55] Barth understood event in terms of the activity of God. Campbell argues that much contemporary theory casts the sermon as an experiential event that has the effect of a happening in itself.

CRITIQUE OF CAMPBELL

So many of Campbell's general criticisms are worthy. When the sermon is open-ended, it can be individualistic. Homiletics has often put too much emphasis on technique that will bring about a transforming experience and not enough emphasis on God. Focus needs to shift from plot to character—the central character of Christ in scripture. Preachers should avoid preaching Jesus as model preacher. Instead of imitating him, they should ensure that he is the one preached. He is not to be explained in anthropological terms, reduced to abstract propositions, or absorbed into general human experience. His relationship to abstract concepts should be rendered narratively. Preachers should be forming a people worthy of the story, not telling a different story more "relevant" to the people. Preachers should ask what the Holy Spirit is saying to the church through scripture. They should allow the church to be the "middle term"[56] in the movement from text to sermon. Campbell wants preachers to engage in "figural interpretation," which is an imaginative act of "seeing narrative patterns and connections between events, people, and institutions" then and now and linking them typologically through immersion in scripture.[57]

Some of the homileticians Campbell criticizes would agree with his criticisms of contemporary preaching and might have been surprised to see themselves cast as opponents. Campbell also elevates the community over against the individual; yet as Lischer and others have stressed, both are essential, and both must respond to the confessional question, "Who do you say that I am?" Campbell also dismisses the narrative movement in preaching because he finds that its emphasis is on stories and experience, not the storied identity of Christ in scripture.

David Lose has made a detailed and important critique of Campbell and the postliberal implications for preaching, notably the primacy given to the world of the Bible over the created world.[58] Still Campbell's contribution is important. He stresses that narrative in itself is not the issue, but the content and ascriptive logic of the biblical narrative, namely it is in praise of Jesus Christ. He wants preaching to be intertextual, not narrowly confined to pericopes. Moreover, he places ecclesiology front and center in homiletics in giving priority in preaching to forming the church and the need of using imagination and typological connections to scripture (Bartlett's "echoes") to do so.

Assessment

Of the six possibilities we have explored here, the first three (Chapell, Hilkert, and African American preaching) are variations of the trouble/grace school and open additional ways of thinking about it and further opportunities for conversation. Charles Bartow and Marjorie Hewitt Suchocki represent distinct alternatives, still conceiving of the Word as event. Charles Campbell represents a postliberal stance that tends to mute God's voice in the preaching event, which is one step toward the radical postmodern homiletic that we will examine in the next section. Other possibilities for theologies of preaching exist beyond the six we have explored, though they are more hinted at than fully developed. They include Gerhard O. Forde's idea of preaching as an act of atonement, though not in the sense of Christ taking our place on the cross. In preaching, Christ enters death ahead of us and brings us to the death we require in order to be remade as a new creation in Christ and to receive the new life God intended us to have all along.[59] Michael Quicke, drawing on James B. Torrance, argues for preaching as a Trinitarian venture instead of as a unitarian one: Most preaching focuses on humans and leaves out the Holy Spirit as well as Christ as mediator and sole priest.[60] Donald English,[61] Craig A. Loscalzo,[62] and David Buttrick independently argue for preaching as an inauguration of the realm (kingdom) of God. Buttrick argues that neoorthodoxy redefined revelation in terms of the Christ event and made the focus of preaching "the past-tenseness of Christ himself."[63] A sense of God-with-us has gone missing. He calls for eschatology not just to inform preaching, but for its vision of the future to assist preachers in preaching boldly about social injustice in the present.

Much more homiletical work needs to be done on theologies of preaching and their implications for sermon structure. Three of the six theologies we have examined fall clearly within the trouble/grace school (or whatever name would be best to give it in its expanded expression). If much African American homiletics belongs within trouble/grace, then the landscape of North American preaching shifts. For too long African American preaching, widely regarded as some of the best in the world today, has sat at the fringes of homiletics. In its various expressions it has been seen as something inimitable, belonging to particular cultures and heritages, unique unto itself, all of which is true, yet for these reasons it has not been fully engaged as a dialogue partner. If much African American preaching belongs within the trouble/grace school, it belongs there because of its underlying theological structure and ways of reading scripture. Trouble/grace is not only a large school, it is arguably the largest school in homiletics today, with relatively few clear alternatives. Trouble/grace was already the only school that is explicitly theological in its approach to sermon form and content. Moreover, if trouble/grace is the school to which much African American homiletics belongs, there is even more reason to be in dialogue with it, to learn from it, and to honor it for its enormous accomplishment. African American homiletics in turn may derive its benefit in further development of its homiletical theory.

It is essential to be engaged in theologies of preaching, for they allow us as preachers to think through what it is that we do and why. They help identify emphases that may be missing in contemporary preaching. Beyond that, theologies of preaching can be a source and guide for homiletical practice. In the next section we continue our consideration of theology from the perspective of practical theology and ethics.

SECTION THREE

PRACTICAL THEOLOGY

1. rhetoric
2. social justice
3. ethics
4. an ethic of preaching
5. character of the preacher
6. pastoral care
7. multiculturalism

Rhetoric

Ronald J. Allen: Persuasive Authority

Ronald J. Allen explores the teaching possibilities of preaching ethics in his *Preaching the Topical Sermon, The Teaching Sermon, Preaching and Practical Ministry,* as well as in a joint book with Barbara Shires Blaisdell and Scott Black Johnston, *Theology for Preaching: Authority, Truth, and Knowledge of God in a Postmodern Ethos.* For Allen, communities see truth differently. Thus notions of authority are currently undermined. Preachers cannot simply present tradition and expect it to be accepted. They must present a rationale for it and identify points at which it can be instructive. In other words, they must be persuasive, and for this rhetoric may be the key. The authority of preaching is established by bringing tradition into dialogue with contemporary experience, presenting material in a conversational manner, respecting other viewpoints, presenting alternative interpretations, and honestly acknowledging ambiguity and uncertainty when they exist. "The sermon becomes authoritative," he says, "to the degree that the conversation about its visions and claims offers promise to the community."[1] One might hope that the sermon becomes authoritative and persuasive largely because it is based in the Word of God, who speaks in and through it, not because it offers a promise. Blaisdell argues that preaching is needed, nonetheless, to foster ethical decisions on the part of listeners. This can be achieved not through coercion, but by the preacher pondering difficult questions, issues, and responsibilities and presenting choices to the congregation.[2] Johnson offers an excellent caution against reducing the authority of preaching to offering a promise to the community. He says that even in our world, when the meaning of authority has become polyvalent, authority remains a faithful term. The authority to preach is the call of Jesus Christ through a community of faith. Preaching has as its content and relevancy the gospel message.[3]

William Willimon: Baptismal Language

William Willimon thought so when he wrote about the "peculiar speech" that preachers employ when they preach to the baptized. The language is baptismal language. Since it is spoken to people who are dying and being raised, it must not be translated into terms the world finds acceptable or that meet individual therapeutic or experiential needs.[4] It is also political speech of "prophetic resistance and reformation."[5] It is the same bold language of the gospel that we are to preach to the unbaptized because, "We really have no idea what is happening to us until we meet the gospel, until the gospel helps us to name our pathologies–pathologies that are so widespread in this culture as to make them appear normal–as bondage to be overcome rather than as fixed, closed reality simply to be accepted."[6] His counsel to be bold in proclamation of the gospel is important: Too often preachers tailor the gospel to what they think people want to hear, when it may not be what they need to hear or what God wants them to hear.

André Resner: Persuasive Effect

André Resner's *Preacher and Cross: Person and Message in Theology and Rhetoric* makes an important statement about rhetoric and the sermon. In the history of preaching, the Latin fathers and twentieth-century Barthians scorned rhetoric, for they deemed it extra-theological. Augustine and many contemporary theorists have argued that rhetoric is important for preaching but is theologically neutral. Resner argues that the two positions represent an impasse in homiletics and offer a false choice. In homiletical rhetoric, persuasion and efficacy are not mere synonyms, as they are typically treated. Persuasion has to do with choices the preacher makes, and efficacy has to do "with confessional faith convictions about God and God's working." God is ultimately in control of preaching.[7]

Rhetoric offers "persuasive effect" to preaching. This is accomplished in large measure by what the listeners perceive in relationship to the preacher's character as shaped by the cross. Some people who have been wounded by life think of or experience the cross as something that compounds individual suffering. Still, it nonetheless remains the power of God for salvation. It "is that power of God which renders evil as evil and which orients one to survive as an agent of redemption in a world 'not yet' fully inhabited by God's shalom, yet one in which it is promised and guaranteed in Jesus' death and resurrection."[8] Theology offers the "efficacy" of the proclaimed gospel for salvation. Both rhetoric and theology, Christian character and content are essential.

Resner thus suggests that we think of ethos not in Aristotelian terms of the speaker's credibility and persuasive ability, but in Pauline terms of "reverse-*ethos*,"[9] who the preacher is and what the preacher needs to do to communicate the Christian message. In other words, the preacher's ethos should not be discerned according to credibility standards in the society or culture, but only from the character of the "cross-event-proclaimed" that orients the community's choices for action and shapes its own character.[10] In this manner of being an example, the preacher offers personal testimony and concrete instances of God's activity of redemption in the world. One could add that the preacher's ethos adds an ethical dimension to everything that is said because of the claim of the cross. Resner's discussion is important not least because it stresses that the efficacy of preaching depends upon its God-centeredness and that rhetoric is its necessary complement—it has to do with the human role in preaching.

Social Justice

Walter J. Burghardt: A Flaming Spirituality for Justice

In *Preaching the Just Word,* his Lyman Beecher Lectures on preaching, Walter J. Burghardt, S.J., argued that the key to the revival of the social gospel is to move beyond homilies that provide important information, skills, and strategies, to a spirituality that sets preachers aflame with concern for justice. Much of North America's Christian culture conceives of the incarnation in individual terms as the forgiveness of sins and the relationship of the individual soul to eternity. Scripture indicates that Christ came also to relieve human suffering in the present. Biblical justice is not mere human justice that is often conceived as equal treatment. Rather justice, as Burghardt defines it, is "appropriate treatment that will equalize the relationship and provide access to resources."[11]

It is not giving what the other deserves, but self-giving, without consideration of the merit of the recipient. In other words, biblical justice is loving as Jesus loved; hence, it is a matter of spiritual discipline. The early Matthean community, at least, understood the great commandment to mean that "it is always Christ" who is hungry or thirsty, naked or a stranger, sick or in prison. Burghardt demonstrates exemplary concern for the poor: Social doctrine, he says, remains a head-trip until it touches "the less fortunate images of Jesus, those who share far more of his crucifixion than of his resurrection."[12]

Burghardt recommends preaching four important social justice principles:

1. "A person is more precious for what he or she is than for what he or she has"; thus we are to share rather than possess.[13]

2. We have a right only to as much of the earth's resources as we need "to live a human existence in union with God."[14]

3. "[T]he real presence of Christ [is] in the unfortunate and underprivileged, in the impoverished and imprisoned, in the maimed and marginalized."[15]

4. "[W]e must proclaim...the reality that binds us to all that is human"; in other words, we exist in community rather than in isolation.[16]

Burghardt is also concerned for "the predicament of the prosperous" like Zacchaeus, then and now.[17] Burghardt argues against preachers using general principles and scriptural slogans that in fact perpetuate injustice. Similarly, a preacher must not dogmatize or pontificate, but be able to listen and to raise issues. As a preacher raising issues, I must "lay them out, even tell my people where I stand and why. Not to impose my convictions as gospel, but to quicken their Christian conscience, spur them to personal reflection."[18] Burghardt raises many social justice issues in this volume and demonstrates how he deals with them in homilies.

Stanley P. Saunders and Charles L. Campbell: The Word as Antidote to Death

Two volumes on social justice deserve special mention. Stanley P. Saunders and Charles L. Campbell have published *The Word on the Street: Performing the Scriptures in the Urban Context*, a powerful account of two professorial colleagues at Columbia Seminary and their work with the homeless in Atlanta. For them the antidote to death is the efficacy of the proclaimed Word. They take their classes in New Testament and preaching out of the safe classrooms of the seminary into the places of the poor to read the Bible from that perspective. The methodological tools they use are the same, but by altering the physical space the students learn an important principle: "where we learn shapes what we learn, and where we read shapes how we read."[19] These authors argue that the homeless perform an essential critical theological function in our society, especially once middle-class folk spend time with them. Then they see various ways in which the "powers that be" enact laws that contribute to their suffering. Local ordinances opposing overnight urban camping and protecting "quality of life" are more often "delusions of death."[20] Preaching on street corners represents what these authors call an "extreme homiletic" that they have engaged outside of their Open Door Community every Wednesday morning after breakfast. None of the institutional or official trappings remain. It is just Word and voice: "absolute trust in the Word of God and faithful stewardship of the human voice."[21] In such settings, the liberating message of the gospel may be experienced anew, though it may not be a Word the world wants to hear. There is a long Christian tradition of outdoor preaching that dates back to the Bible. It would be helpful to hear Saunders and Campbell reflect on what is lost in their own experience of such preaching by being not just outside and separated from the supporting structures of regular worship, but perhaps also being perceived as outside of a church, outside of an accountable community, or outside of where the world may be willing to hear.

Kathy Black: Preaching and Disability

Finally, Kathy Black brings a fresh perspective to homiletics in both her *A Healing Homiletic: Preaching and Disability* and a subsequent essay on that topic.[22] She considers the implications of preaching on Jesus' healing ministry for those who suffer disabilities today. She herself suffers from a disability and has worked with persons with various disabilities. A preacher's unexamined attitudes and use of language can cause additional suffering for those with disability today.

Black challenges both literal interpretations of miracle stories that equate disability with sin and metaphorical interpretations (e.g., we all need our blindness healed) that treat disabilities as negative terms. When Jesus' miracle stories are applied to today, for instance, in a sermon or a healing service, it is often with the expectation of a cure. "[M]iraculous cures can happen," but when cure becomes the pastor's goal, "the persons with the disabilities often do not feel accepted *as they are*."[23] This can be the source of much pain. Such expectations of a cure can deny or ignore healings of various sorts that fall short of a cure. Black prefers healing services to focus on healing in the midst of disability, for instance the healing of broken relationships and isolation. Fractured relationships are the most difficult aspects of living with physical disability, she says. Many persons with a disability do not summarize their existential reality as suffering. She wants preachers to nurture communities of interdependence that value the gifts of each person, where all people are agents of the miraculous transformations that God wills for each human life.

Five excellent preaching guidelines emerge from Black:

1. Avoid using disabilities as metaphors. Instead, state clearly the intended message (e.g., instead of "we are blind," say, "we do not understand who Jesus is").

2. Look at the situation of the person with the disability in the biblical text, rather than focus on the disability itself.

3. Acknowledge the many cultural and social boundaries Jesus crossed in performing many of his healings.

4. Emphasize the actions of the person with the disability in the text.

5. Focus on the response of the crowds.[24]

The church at times does not seem much ahead of the rest of society in dealing with people of differing abilities, and preachers need the insights Black and others have to offer.

Other Contributions

Several volumes have recently been written on social justice and preaching, including one by Arthur Van Seters entitled *Preaching and Ethics*,[25] which is in the present series, but was not yet available to me when writing this. Other volumes include a dutiful if uninspiring reminder of the importance of preaching justice from systematic theologian James M. Childs;[26] a fine collection of essays on ethnic and cultural perspectives of justice edited by Christine M. Smith;[27] and insightful essays on sexual and domestic violence, edited by John S. McClure and Nancy J. Ramsay.[28] Teachers of preaching who want to design a course on social justice might consult two Roman Catholic priests who collaborated in a project for the Association of Theological Schools. They determine how students might be motivated to begin developing their "public characters" as ministers of the Word "in a world needing the Gospel infused with justice."[29]

Ethical Method

For reasons too deep to probe here, homileticians in so-called mainline denominations tend to equate ethics with social justice and ignore individual ethics. In evangelical circles, the situation is reversed, while in much African American homiletics the two most often are fruitfully united. However, significant help is now being offered to preachers on ethical method from various places in the theological perspective. David P. Gushee and Robert H. Long, *A Bolder Pulpit:*

Reclaiming the Moral Dimension of Preaching, is a helpful book on the preaching of ethics from an evangelical perspective.[30] They offer a fine methodology for doing ethics. The best preparation for moral preaching, they say, is a broad theological base and wide reading in biblical themes, motifs, doctrines, and narratives. They encourage the preacher to engage in a calculated movement from a theological framework through the following:

1. Broad statements of moral conviction or principles. ("Principles do not tell one directly and concretely what to do or not to do, but provide the underlying basis for many rules that do exactly that."[31])

2. Moral rules that must follow from the principles, because it is easy to hide behind principles and do nothing. (The principle of neighbor love leads to the rules, "do not retaliate; forgive one another." The principle of justice leads to the rules, "do not take bribes; act on behalf of the stranger."[32])

3. Particular moral judgments in a specific congregation, such as, "forgive the man who burned our church" or "protest the treatment plant in a low-income area."[33] (These do not carry the same moral weight as principles and rules because the preacher may be wrong.)

When someone in the congregation challenges a particular rule, the principle behind it should be explained. If ethical principles conflict, preachers are to seek a foundation in "the character, conduct and will of God" and in the broad theological framework.[34] These authors maintain that one reason for the numerical success of many evangelical congregations is their moral clarity.[35]

Using the four norms of moral conviction these authors encourage preachers to ask two additional questions: For whom? (Who is my audience?) About what? (What issues should the moral arena address in the sermon?) Is the sermon about what people should believe and teach; individual and community character, i.e., who we are to be; or moral practice and behaviors we are to perform?[36] Perhaps one of the best features of this approach is that it provides a distinctive method preachers may follow. It is not simply a rule-based ethics of the sort that removes thinking, and that too often focuses only on the individual.

John R. Bisagno: Principle Preaching

John R. Bisagno's *Principle Preaching* is a variation on what Rick Warren of Saddleback Community Church in Mission Viejo,

California, advocates in his "purpose driven" teachings. Instead of using sermon points it draws principles from the Bible that can be applied to life and illustrated. The principles themselves are the points of the sermon. Thus a four-point sermon on the call, command, conquest, and courage of Joshua 1:1–7 becomes instead broad claims about the present under which the biblical text will be discussed: (1) Don't get stuck in life's passageways; (2) God's already been where you are going; (3) God has a wonderful blueprint for your life; and (4) Yesterday's faithfulness guarantees tomorrow's courage.[37] The principles are derived from what the points say by way of application to life. Bisagno apparently has not read much homiletics or postmodern theology, and he remains confident that such principles are universal and will be received universally.[38] Still, this is an intriguing approach, particularly in his dynamic way of converting points into principles, and in retaining a God focus in the principles.

An Ethic of Preaching

Not all homileticians agree that preaching principles in this manner is necessarily the way to go. Some ask, Is there an ethic implicit in the act of preaching itself?[39]

Charles L. Campbell: An Ethical Performance of Jesus' Way

Charles L. Campbell takes a similar departure from preaching ethics by principles in his *The Word Before the Powers: An Ethic of Preaching.* Preaching on social issues is important at times but it also presents three problems. It assumes that

1. people can solve social ills if they are of good will and work together;
2. "the ethical dimensions of preaching [are] much broader than principles of decision-making;" and
3. more important than principles is the daily shaping of a community of character.[40]

Jesus chose to preach, and for Campbell this implies an ethic for preaching, simply in the *that* of preaching as opposed to the *what.*[41] Campbell claims that preaching involves an ethical performance of Jesus' way of preaching, "the way of active, nonviolent resistance to and engagement with the principalities and powers of the world."[42] The *what* of preaching has often participated in the "Domination System" by supporting wars, slavery, racism, sexism, and the economic status quo.[43] Campbell adopts Christine M. Smith's call for preaching active resistance[44] instead of simple transformation, because "the language of resistance takes more seriously the enormity of the principalities and powers."[45] He calls for proclamation of a redemptive word, and for privileged congregations that are not oppressed this means "redemption from captivity" rather than "liberation from oppression."[46]

Preaching Jesus Christ is central, for "human weakness before the powers always reminds us that we rely on the power of God, not our own strength, in resistance."[47] In proclaiming Christ the principalities and powers are exposed, and the new creation is already breaking into the fallen world. This new creation "is inseparable from Jesus, in whose life, death and resurrection the new creation is both present and coming. Jesus himself confronts his hearers with a new reality, which challenges their ways of seeing the world."[48] Campbell makes brief but important claims about God's role in preaching resistance. Even more attention to this would further guard his ethic from being seen as something that we do and are capable of doing, an ethic that is simple moralizing.

Campbell's book is important because it casts all preaching as ethical. He presents an important challenge for each sermon: Does it in fact contribute to a community of moral character? He recommends the following preaching practices:

1. redescribe the practices of the church in terms of resistance to the powers;

2. articulate and expose unconscious social practices, and show how the church has "accommodated to the powers of death, causing [it] to act as a fallen power," and

3. cultivate intentional practices of discipleship and community formation that embody resistance.[49]

Campbell's adoption of the term *resistance* to describe Christian character may be good in that it implies a stark alternative: We either resist, or we comply with the powers and principalities. Resistance is a good adjective for the postmodern ethos, which resists all unexamined authority, as we will see in the next chapter. Still, one could wish for a better word. *Resistance* is hardly adequate to describe the Christian ethos or character: it implies that Christian living is primarily in response to the powers, which is problematic for several reasons.

First, Christian life is in response to the graciousness and goodness of God and creation, not to how bad the world is. Second, resistance implies that the initiative lies with the powers, as indeed often it does, but it dominantly lies with God and with Christ's disciples empowered by the Holy Spirit. Third, the ethos of Christ's preaching is not easily summed up as resistance, and even the attempt to do so is suspect. When the powers stand before the Word, verbs such as *unmasks* and *overthrows* offer more apt descriptions of what actually transpires.

The Character of the Preacher

From the Enlightenment until the mid 1800s, the character of the preacher was a common topic in homiletics. Only lately is it starting to return with the returning influence of rhetoric.[50] Lucy Hogan and Robert Reid devote a chapter to the preacher's persona from the perspective of rhetoric.[51] André Resner considers the preacher's character from the perspective of rhetoric and theology.[52] Charles Campbell approaches from the perspective of a spirituality of nonviolent resistance, concentrating on particular practices and virtues, namely: friendship, truthfulness, anger, patience, and hope.[53] By far the greatest area of concentration of literature on the character of the preacher concerns women. Mary Catherine Hilkert devotes a chapter to women and preaching from a Roman Catholic perspective.[54] Mary Donovan Turner and Mary Lin Hudson,[55] Christine M. Smith,[56] and Carol M. Norén[57] have all written books on the subject of justice and women. Still, not a lot has been written on the character of the preacher. This is surprising because of (a) the high incidence of women who leave the ministry, suggesting inadequacies in the manner in which seminaries prepare women for ministry, (b) the lack of pastoral support they usually receive from their denominations once they have graduated, and (c) the high number of court cases involving clergy malpractice in all denominations.

Pastoral Care

G. Lee Ramsey: The Individual within a Community

Just as Campbell claims that all sermons imply ethics, so too, G. Lee Ramsey's *Care-full Preaching* claims that all sermons are pastoral. He laments that pastoral preaching is associated with therapeutic preaching in which the pastoral concern for the hearer has "shrunk the grand and awesome mystery of God-with-us down to the miniature size of the individual psyche."[58] Instead of addressing the inward struggle of the believer, pastoral preaching appropriately considers the location of the individual within a community of believers in a particular time and place.

Pastoral care takes place in sermons in particular in the way they represent:

1. Theological Anthropology: What does the sermon say about:
   a. who we are as human beings (i.e., about human nature and sin and human responsibility) and
   b. the sustenance and healing that God provides (i.e., about God's grace and human freedoms and limits)?
2. Ecclesiology: How is the church construed as a pastoral community in the world? Ramsey uses this question to reflect on the pastoral dimensions of sermons.[59]

His model (especially item 1, above) falls within the trouble/grace school and joins Campbell in its focus on ecclesiology. In fact, if one combines Campbell's three recommendations for ethical preaching (concerning his *The Word Before the Powers,* previously) with Ramsey's recommendations for pastoral preaching, one ends up with a very significant checklist on the prophetic and pastoral dimensions of preaching.

Edward P. Wimberly: Moving from Shame to Self-Worth

Two other recent books deserve attention for their approaches to pastoral preaching. Edward P. Wimberly is concerned with uniting preaching and pastoral counseling in his *Moving from Shame to Self-Worth: Preaching and Pastoral Care.*[60] As an African American, Wimberly says that he experiences shame whenever a member of his ethnic and racial group is devalued. He points to many others who experience shame daily, for example, those who have been sexually abused or who are addicted to drugs or alcohol. His proposal for sermons parallels what he does in counseling: He explores Jesus' words for what they say about himself, his relationships, and his ministry; particularly around the issues of shame and self-worth. After finding a "mimetic lesson" or paradigm about shame in the biblical text, he uses it to provide focus in retelling the biblical story such that in hearing it a person suffering from shame experiences Jesus dealing with it in the text.

Wimberly also seeks a parallel story in contemporary events to further embody that encounter today. His stories are powerful, and his way of retelling biblical stories to involve those needing care can serve as a model for preachers in any tradition, perhaps not every Sunday, but from time to time.

Robert C. Dykstra: Attention to One's Own Interests and Desires

The most unusual pastoral offering focuses on preachers caring better for themselves in preparing sermons. Robert C. Dykstra teaches pastoral theology at Princeton Seminary and does not allow an apparent absence of reading in homiletics to deter him from his project. His idiosyncratic *Discovering a Sermon: Personal Pastoral Preaching,* uses the psychoanalysis of D. W. Winnicott to instruct preachers in preparing a pastoral sermon: "One learns what to preach in large measure through sustained attention to one's interests and desires; one learns how to preach in large measure through imitating others."[61]

For Dykstra, the biblical text should be treated in the same way that a teddy bear is treated by a child, as a transitional object that is to be played with now and that will be left behind when it no longer has emotional or other significance. He pleads for preachers to allow "a willingness to create and to be re-created again and again in relation to a beloved object."[62] He encouraged a student who had seen a black squirrel to free-associate about it for fifteen minutes to an hour as part of preparing to preach. This provided a way to engage the depths of his own life and lives around him.[63] In the privacy of their study preachers are to track their own mundane interests and desires, the preacher's "mundane squirrel" (not a teddy bear after all)–"to the point of being threatened by it with sadness, pain, or hope; of questioning prior actions or beliefs; or of finding oneself in tears, or with an irregular heartbeat or sweaty palms, even sexually aroused."[64] By this process preachers will be led to stories to preach. Dykstra is nothing if not brave, yet his sermons do seem more integrated, head and heart, than many published sermons one reads.

Preaching in a Multicultural Setting

Homiletics began moving to hearer-centered preaching more than three decades ago. For many years, preachers assumed that a congregation was uniform because everyone lived in one culture, American, Canadian, British, French, or whatever. Kathy Black and Christine Smith have led the way in calling preachers to attend to the needs of those who for reasons of health, disability, gender, sexual orientation, ethnic origin, race, age, or class are not made to feel at home through the sermon.

Lenora Tubbs Tisdale: A Congregation's Many Cultures

One of the first people in homiletics to attend to the postmodern reality that there are often many cultures in a congregation is Lenora Tubbs Tisdale. In *Preaching as Local Theology and Folk Art,* she devised principles for doing exegesis of a congregation. This is a novel idea, even though preachers since Paul and Augustine, especially those who have paid attention to rhetoric, have been attentive to whom they are preaching in one way or another. For Tubbs Tisdale, preaching is a "hearer-oriented event."[65] She wants preachers to be attentive to the various subcultures in a congregation and to listen to the many "resident theologians" who "contribute to the questions, insights, struggles, and life situations that feed the formation of the Sunday sermon."[66] These are the people who can help the preacher render the sermon in local contextual theology, grounded in the lives and experiences of the congregation.

Her method of cultural analysis is rooted in "thick description" and local events as signs and symbols. These are to be treated as "texts." The preacher can draw material from: stories and interviews, archival resources, demographics, architecture and visual arts, rituals, events and activities, and various people.[67] The next exegetical step is analysis and interpretation of the cultural data with particular attention to worldview and values (e.g., views of God, humanity, creation, time or eschatology, church, mission) and ethos.[68] Tubbs Tisdale conceives of the sermon as imaginative "dance" or as folk art in which the preacher as local theologian imaginatively discerns "fitting and faithful themes for proclamation." The preacher as folk artist seeks "symbols, forms, and movements that are capable of capturing and transforming the imaginations of a particular local community of faith."[69] This kind of community exegesis is not what a preacher needs to undertake week by week, for the congregation does not change that rapidly. But it is the kind of exercise preachers should undertake occasionally and for special services, and should at least mentally engage each week in preparing sermons.

Joseph R. Jeter Jr. and Ronald J. Allen: One Gospel, Many Ears

Lenora Tubbs Tisdale's book has led the way for other books on multiculturalism, two of particular note. Joseph R. Jeter Jr. and Ronald J. Allen, in *One Gospel, Many Ears: Preaching for Different Listeners in the Congregation,* have written on a range of hearer-related subjects. These include varieties of listeners, different generations, different modes of mental process, gender issues, ability issues, and preaching to a mixture of conservatives and liberals. This is a useful volume for an age in which many people attend seminary without background in the church. What might seem like wisdom and common sense to those reared in the church may seem novel or innovative to those from outside. With regard to preaching in multicultural settings, these authors offer helpful guidance: Preachers need to help congregations become genuinely multicultural, grieve the loss of their old identity, and "envision the gospel qualities of a multicultural church and world."[70] In such settings "one size fits all" sermons may not work; they advocate "perichoretic"[71] circular dance models (the awkwardness of this term, even with its Trinitarian echo, makes one wish for a better one) that engage themes and texts from more than a single perspective.[72]

James R. Nieman and Thomas G. Rogers: Cross-Cultural Strategies

James R. Nieman and Thomas G. Rogers conducted hundreds of interviews with experienced pastors in multicultural congregations. They used these interviews as the basis of *Preaching to Every Pew: Cross-Cultural Strategies*. They recommend that preachers in their own settings imitate the interview processes that they themselves followed. By considering culture through various "frames"—ethnicity, class, displacement, and beliefs—they assemble a reliable portrait of a congregational setting. Their study has implications for the preacher, who must become aware of his or her own cultural limitations, as well as those of the sermon.

Sermon preparation in multicultural settings needs to be collaborative, involving members of the congregation in Bible study and in choice of images or stories; this study offers limited support to the roundtable approaches of John McClure and Lucy Rose that we will examine in the next chapter.[73] The sermon must "presume mutuality in how meaning is constructed"[74] and is often best followed by a discussion that allows other voices and perspectives to be heard. Moreover, for sermons to connect with hearers, the congregation first has to practice hospitality toward others through initial greetings, church structure, and participation.

In sermons, preachers emphasize not differences but what is shared: There is no greater element in common than life in Jesus Christ. Cross-cultural sermons thus culminate in a joyous celebration of God as the giver of life and as the One who can be trusted in all things.[75] When they attended to culture, preachers found that whatever sermon forms they explored, the sermon, by its very form signaled, "an encounter with God in which memory is reconstructed, experiences are affirmed, and dignity is conferred."[76] By being open to cultural differences, preachers found that congregations are more attentive to the wider world beyond the church and that the sermon is seen as a witness to God's mission of "divine generosity whose trajectory has a cosmic sweep."[77] Nieman and Rogers concentrated on multicultural preaching, but they have provided homiletics with some of the first documented evidence of what makes for effective preaching in such settings.

In this chapter we have considered a wide range of publications that deal with ethical matters and preaching, and we have considered them in the categories of rhetoric, social justice, ethical method, an ethic of preaching, character of the preacher, pastoral care, and multiculturalism. We have seen tensions within our discussion: Should preaching strive to be persuasive by rhetorical standards, or should the persuasive effect of preaching arise out of the preaching of the cross? Can attention to how one's message will be heard remove the power of the gospel to affect social change from one's preaching? Should ethics be primarily based in rules and principles that tend to focus on individuals, or should it be based in formation of an ethical community? Are these false alternatives? Do social demands of the faith require preaching to move outside of church buildings, and when it is in church buildings, ought it be primarily understood as resistance to the powers of the world? Can a preacher take care of the needs of a congregation if she or he is not aware of her or his own needs? Can preaching be either ethical or pastoral if it does not take account of the demographic composition of the congregation? These and other important ethical questions have been raised in these significant writings, but there has been a notable absence of writing to consider ethical global issues in preaching. It is now time in a concluding chapter to consider one school of ethical thought that has emerged in homiletics that demands attention, not only for what it represents by way of a positive ethic, but also for the problems it may pose by its radical postmodern stance.

9

POSTMODERN OR RADICAL POSTMODERN?

An Ethic for Homiletics

Ethics in preaching cannot be reduced to ethical rules. Everything that preachers do implies ethics: how they talk about faith, appeal to authority, discuss individual and corporate moral character, analyze social situations, as well as appeal to norms, standards, values, and principles.[1] In this final chapter we deal with an ethic for homiletics that can be no less broad. Some homileticians may be loosely grouped into a major ethical school that may be called the radical postmodern school. It appropriately leans in the direction of welcoming those people who are strangers, marginalized, or outsiders, particularly those who feel excluded for one reason or another from the church. However, it does so at some cost. We will first consider this school and then explore some alternative directions.

The Radical Postmodern School

Terms and Their Meanings

First, we need to deal with a confusion of terms. Increasingly writers describe homiletics with terms like New Homiletic, postmodern, postcritical, postliberal, and even post-Christian. In the present fast-paced world we are post-something, and much of the discussion in homiletics concerns just what that "something" is. The postmodern age can be characterized as decentered and dispersing. This post-something mind-set favors, among other things:

1. horizontal ideas of authority
2. the social system rather than the individual
3. interdependence over independence
4. relationship over autonomy
5. communication ahead of information
6. multiple meanings and interpretations rather than singular
7. the absence of closure

The postmodern influence in homiletics has been largely positive, not least in language theory and narrative, in raising concern for the marginalized, and in breaking the hegemony of historical criticism by allowing literary and other readings of the Bible to come to the fore. The postmodern generally stands not for anarchy and the absence of meaning, but for the excess of meaning. In other words, too many individuals and schools of thought are raising too many competing claims in the interpretation of texts. Thus any one claim that seeks to establish itself over others in a privileged position without being open to critique becomes a problem. The objective truth claims of modernity are rejected. A different kind of truth claim has emerged. This claim relates entirely to perspective. On the negative side, postmodernity can serve as an ideology that is inherently anarchic, de-stabilizing, anti-communal, de-constructive, opposing any kind of foundation, without at the same time calling for anything positive.[2] That is its danger, yet it also holds rich possibility. How one negotiates competing claims in postmodern times is critical.

Ronald J. Allen, Barbara Shires Blaisdell, and Scott Black Johnston offer a fine homiletical introduction to the subject of the postmodern in preaching.[3] They focus on what it is like to preach when so much of the culture is shifting. Johnson's contribution stood out in that volume because he voiced appropriate caution against faith being turned into a belief in postmodernism. In 1994, Robert Stephen Reid[4] wrote that the New Homiletic, in other words homiletics since 1965, "is not a radical postmodern approach...[but it is] commensurate with much of the postmodern."[5] More recent essays by Reid and Lucy Lind Hogan, Eugene Lowry, Alyce McKenzie, Jeffrey Bullock, and James W. Thompson see the postmodern and the New Homiletic as identical.[6] I take contemporary homiletics, New Homiletic, and postmodern homiletics to be synonyms. They refer to sermons with the following characteristics:

1. engage the experience of the hearers
2. seek to confirm rather than to prove
3. value concrete experience over abstraction
4. conceive of form as an extension and expression of content[7]
5. are often inductive and employ narrative
6. allow for participation and disagreement

Currently several homileticians are writing about ethics. While they are quite different in many respects, they have enough in common, without being uniform, to be considered loosely as a new school of homiletics. Most of the members of this school refer to themselves as postmodern, but another term may be necessary, especially if the postmodern is identified with what has transpired in homiletics over the last few decades. Members of this school include John McClure, Joseph M. Webb, Christine M. Smith, L. Susan Bond, and Lucy Rose.[8] (Although McClure includes Charles Campbell in this group, I do not, because I see his position as being significantly different.[9]) Rose and McClure[10] claim that homiletics has now moved beyond New Homiletic to the postmodern stances that they represent, though all would say that they have benefited greatly from it, and not all would seem to distance themselves from it in this way. In other words, this version of the postmodern is not necessarily an ally of the New Homiletic. Thus we may need to distinguish between their stance, which I call radical, not just because Christine Smith encourages it[11], but because they establish their ethic for the pulpit largely by leaving God out of the discussion.

Ethics can be and often is preaching, but it is not usually proclamation. It typically is not accompanied by a preaching of the gospel, however we may define that, and it does not in most churches lead to an encounter with God. The key homiletical problem is that ethics puts human behavior front and center, while, for what I am calling proclamation, God needs to be front and center. What God has done and is doing in Jesus Christ and through the Holy Spirit is of greatest significance, and what we do as human beings is necessarily seen in light of that. When preaching is proclamation, the sermon is performative, not just informative. It does things, not just because we know that language in general does things in and of itself, but because in and through the sermon God speaks the Word that God fulfills. It has the eventful quality of revelation, encounter, and meeting one's Savior. What we do by way of ethics is an appropriate response to the gospel, an essential response, an empowered response. Here I want to claim that only linked with the gospel can ethics be proclamation and that so linked it is more radical, in Smith's positive sense of that term, than ethics on its own—it is more radical because it is transformative.

BOLD CLAIMS

The radical postmodern school raises timely important issues; yet to my mind, its solutions often raise more problems than they answer—which may be part of this school's constructive purpose. While its members do not uniformly hold all of the positions I will name, here are some of their more significant bold claims, some aspects of which are to be applauded:

Avoid Hierarchy. The radical postmodernists seek to avoid hierarchy in preaching. For Webb, this is primarily a desire to avoid sermons that are monologues instead of conversations, that make no real connection with the people in the pews.[12] Lucy Rose, in *Sharing the Word: Preaching in the Roundtable Church,* sought to avoid hierarchy by rotating weekly the responsibility for preaching within the congregation, thereby allowing different perspectives and "wagers." For Rose, the church apparently already knows the gospel and can represent it faithfully, a position that might seem to obviate the necessity for the church to receive the Word. The word *preacher* for her is not a synonym for ordained minister: "[I]t refers to the one whose function for the particular service of worship is to offer the sermon as one exchange in the ongoing conversations of the community."[13]

McClure's *The Roundtable Pulpit*[14] is related to Rose's roundtable: He thinks that preaching should be the result of a collaborative process, in which the preacher meets weekly face to face with a congregational group (for no more than three months per group) to help bring various perspectives into the sermon. McClure is aware that perceptions of hierarchy are not so easily dodged. As long as the church values educated ministry, some type of hierarchy in preaching will persist. The way to proceed may be not to abnegate authority but to use it wisely. He wants to ensure that ethics is part of every appeal to authority in the pulpit. I would argue that when preachers center their preaching on God so that the sermon is experienced as an event of God, not of the preacher, God's authority, not the preacher's, is evident and welcomed. Moreover, ethics in such a setting has the possibility of being not merely informative but transformative.

Deconstruct Authorities. The radical postmodernists are radically for the marginalized. Smith focuses on lesbian, gay, bisexual, and transgendered people who are normally excluded from the church. Webb's focus is sociological and rooted in symbolic interaction social theory; he is concerned with the practical real identity of the generalized or specific "others" who encounter us as strangers every day. His goal is to get beyond the stereotypical and prejudicial definitions we tend to impose upon them.[15] McClure's concept of others is rooted in theological anthropology, in the face-to-face encounter of asking and learning that necessarily precedes speaking for anyone or offering guidance. His other, like Webb's, extends beyond those marginalized by the church community to the singular and particular features of those who in many ways might be strangers: Indeed, he seeks "the glory of the Infinite" in the other.[16]

Preaching is undergoing a deconstruction of its common authorities, namely Bible, tradition, experience, and reason.[17] Deconstruction of the sort that does not "reject the facticity"[18] of these authorities can keep preaching "critically and ethically open and renewable."[19] For McClure preaching is what keeps these authorities renewable for Christian experience and practice. Deconstruction can be understood as a process of "exiting" former identity that allows for the rebirth of preaching as "other-wise,"[20] reoriented toward the "other." He situates preaching as "a radical act of compassionate responsibility."[21] Using the deconstruction theory of Emmanuel Levinas, McClure considers the way the Bible is both centrifugal–fostering identity–and centripetal–problematizing "all positions and identities" and placing all our identities under "erasure" in a manner that allows the Bible to function as scripture by bringing us into proximity with others in a relationship of being for them.[22]

McClure's application of Levinas's "exiting" to preaching creates a difficult schema that seems not to be readily geared for the preacher, yet he is trying to preserve preaching from those who would not be concerned for the other(s). Here is roughly how exiting works for McClure. Preachers are to conceive of five different kinds of memory: The *kerygmatic memory* of tradition is formed centrifugally around certain markers, or *topoi*, like resurrection or transfiguration. What one does with these topical markers is largely personal, for each preacher uses them as building blocks around which he or she imaginatively reconstructs the past. The preacher cannot get back to the original biblical scenes and rather invents a picture or impression of them that takes certain precedence over the words on the canonical page when the preacher is composing a sermon and trying to evoke meaning.[23]

Each of these markers serves to coordinate a flux of memories, longings, and unfulfilled desires. We organize the past around these markers.[24] Kerygmatic memory leads in preaching to *mimetic memory* that at one level–Paul Ricoeur's mimesis$_1$–functions by making analogies between the biblical text and contemporary life. At another level–Ricoeur's mimesis$_2$–*imitative memory* mimics within the sermon the shape and function of the biblical text. Mimetic memory is doomed to fail since it can never be the thing imitated.[25] Yet a fourth kind of memory, *memory as historical reconstruction,* brings official versions of the past to interact with the above kinds of memory and yields history in the sermon.[26] Within memory as historical reconstruction resides the fifth kind of memory, *countermemory*. It looks not just for the kerygmatic version of events but also for the opposing marginalized voices of people who were silenced in the process because their stance was different from those in power: "In other words, countermemory begins to recuperate memory's other(s) from beyond memory's thresholds."[27] Once the preacher starts to encounter these people as real men, women, and children, they need to be taken into account, thereby releasing "an awareness of memory-positions that are, or could be, otherwise."[28] Thus preachers will exit the house of memory that existed on the "originary scene of representation"[29]: "the anamnesis of the church moves toward its others; and preaching, the steward, but no longer the caretaker of the house of memory, becomes otherwise preaching."[30] Said plainly, once one is aware of the needs of those who have been ignored by history, one revises one's version of history accordingly.

In this model, scripture functions in a dominantly social manner and seems to de-emphasize revelation. McClure nonetheless makes an important ethical claim: The church has not allowed the voices of many people to be heard that need to be heard–not just the disenfranchised, women, the poor, gays and lesbians, people with differing abilities. He is concerned that preaching be cautious in its use of appeal to any of its usual authorities to avoid repressing any kind of "difference, novelty, relativity, and openness."[31] The radical postmodernists can help all of homiletics to become more open to others. This includes the global others, the two-thirds of the world who are not privileged. Too much of our preaching is confined to regional or national boundaries.

Minimize Transcendence. The radical postmodern group (apart from Smith), in the works I am citing, seems to minimize transcendence without denying it. They avoid use of the word *truth* to describe what is preached: They prefer other words, such as "*wager,* *working hypothesis, practice,* or *testimonial affirmation* (Rose [and L. Susan Bond], McClure, Campbell, and [Anna Carter] Florence respectively)."[32] Some may be saying that they do not feel confident speaking a truth from God, given our finite and sinful natures as humans. They wish to be humble in their claims. Others may be saying that they are betting their lives on a particular claim, while stopping short of making it universal. All would claim that truth in some sense is communicated through preaching. Meaning and truth are a result of one's social location and ways of knowing—notions of meaning and truth may reflect the importance one gives to an idea as opposed what they represent. To say that language is non-referential means that it points beyond itself with difficulty. There is no reality that we can access apart from language. Truth therefore is always conditional. Such a view of language is helpful and instructive, particularly when dealing with social constructs, since many of our assumptions and attitudes are determined by culture. As preachers we also need to be tentative in many of our claims about God, particularly concerning how our knowledge of God translates into specific social action from one cultural setting to another. However, some radical postmodernists either close the skylight to the transcendent too quickly, or they do not discuss it sufficiently.[33] Their language theory accommodates easily a notion of God who is accessed in and through our language system. However, their theory does not clearly account for the notion of a God who is truth and who is capable of transcending even the limits of our language to impart knowledge and revelation. Were preachers to move in this direction, they might never be able to dispense Gerhard Forde's and Richard Jensen's notion of "proclamation," first and second person direct declarative speech from God, much less speak of God in significant ways.

Represent an Ethic that Diminishes God. Related to the above claim, the radical postmodernists in the works I am citing represent an ethic that at times seems to diminish God. It is often a theology from below (to use Susan Bond's language),[34] generally to the diminution of theology from above.[35] For Christine M. Smith, radical evil is "the pervasive world reality,"[36] and it "dominates our everyday reality."[37] Her *Risking the Terror: Resurrection in This Life*[38] is deep in compassion and redemptive purpose. Resurrection life, she rightly says, has to do with committing ourselves to those who suffer, with "placing our lives in all those places where human beings suffer and are oppressed."[39] Given the topic, I suggest that God is diminished by not exploring in depth the resurrection of Jesus Christ and by focusing mostly on human activity: The "primary focus of my work is not upon the resurrection of Jesus...[but] on the power and possibility of resurrection life in our world today."[40] By resurrection Smith means:

> I believe resurrection life to be of God. It is the undefeatable, eternal power of life that God has offered humanity, and infused into humanity, from the beginning of creation. It is the power of life that raised Jesus from the dead. It is the power of life that raised up the early Christian community. It is the power of life that raises up individuals and whole communities today. Resurrection is offered and given as sheer gift. Yet, at the same time, I believe there are human decisions we make, and actions we take, that can bring us closer to that power and nearer to the possibility of resurrection for all God's people and for creation itself.[41]

I would welcome more focus on Christ here, for these questions are raised for me: Has God done something unique in Jesus or does he demonstrate a principle that is inherent in "the power of life"? Is resurrection an appropriate synonym for the reign of God, or is it better to reserve the term for a unique act in history that has eternal significance?[42] Is it wise to say that, "Jesus became the Resurrected One in the Garden of Gethsemane" by his facing truth and death[43]– given that in Luke 9:51 he turns to Jerusalem and in John he is the Truth? Does resurrection lose its distinctive significance if it is something not only that God does but that we do: "The act of remembering resurrects people, creates energy, vision, and life to change the present and helps us live differently in the future"?[44] Does the statement, "I do not believe that the historical Jesus exclusively embodies the Christ of faith,"[45] imply that the two can be separate, that the Jesus who sat and ate with the sinners is not also the risen and ascended Christ who comes to us in and through the Holy Spirit?

John McClure in *Other-Wise Preaching* makes little reference to the Divine. His program finally resolves into four practical and worthy theological expressions in sermons. The "homiletical payoff" of his theory appears in four areas: the social gospel, liberation theology, *Christus Victor* theology, and theology of victimization. Important though these are, even Gustav Aulen's *Christus Victor* theology joins the other theological payoffs in being anthropocentric. Preachers employing it apparently do not have an experience of the resurrected Christ. They have "an experience of the resurrection community"; they "feel deeply that they are part of a countercultural Christian resistance movement (Christ's body) that is, in no uncertain terms, at war with the structural forces of oppression, violence, and greed in the world."[46] Still, as McClure says, "No matter what form it takes, other-wise commitment feels deeply the proximity of human others and the nearness of an impending alternative reign of God in which things are indeed Other-wise,"[47] thus the issue here may be lack of emphasis on the Divine. Beyond solidarity he means "decisive, existential caring" that may involve advocacy, intervention, taking sides, street-preaching, public witness, and other forms of risk-taking or other-wise preaching.[48] McClure is dreaming about possibilities. Such preaching may not be all that he has in mind, but typically it is removed from a worship context, is not overtly based in scripture, and need have no connection with ordered ministry and the sacraments. He opens many theological issues for discussion.

Imply Theology Is Metaphor without Metaphysical Meaning. For Bond and Webb, in differing ways, theology seems to be metaphor without metaphysical meaning. Joseph M. Webb understands pluralism as the larger umbrella under which postmodernism belongs.[49] Many of the ideas he has been working on for three decades are now being affirmed. He found these ideas in process theologians including Alfred North Whitehead and John Cobb, and in symbolic interaction theorists like George Herbert Mead and John Dewey. All of our religious symbols without exception are symbolic constructs. We want them to be factual and absolute, "yet realistically, they are not. No matter…how many individuals may, in a sense, 'hold them in common,' they are relative symbols and symbol systems."[50] He counsels that we do not need to get upset when someone denies one of our "hub symbols," like the divinity of Christ. Rather we can track the symbol in our own experience to its social origin and use the insight we gain to understand the other person.[51] We believe what we believe because we are socially conditioned to believe it. In his view the Bible is not "'gospel' in any kind of metaphysical sense…instead [it] is the Christian Church's 'charter,' its mythic foundational document. It is not historically true, nor was it even designed to be in its various bits and pieces."[52] Webb seems to reduce the authority of the Bible to our own need for the heart of the faith to be true:

> [T]he absoluteness of such [former] theological assertions, whatever they be, has been a mirage. What we have believed, particularly about Jesus, we can continue to believe as a way to give spiritual meaning and substance to the lives we live.

We can even take our beliefs as ultimate for our own lives, as we choose to do. But it is no longer tenable for us to assert our beliefs about Jesus—about divinity, about resurrection, about his being the only path to God—as final, complete, and unalterable for every human being everywhere.[53]

Webb is pointing to the difficulties we face when we try to communicate our faith, especially to those of other faiths. He believes that presenting "absolute theological assertions" does not work; the mirage may well be our belief that it did or it does. Webb is right to demonstrate sensitivity about how and when best to share our faith, yet if the gospel message is not for everyone, then who is it for, and what standards will determine who is worthy to receive it and who is not? These issues need clarification.

L. Susan Bond understands theology "from below" to be rooted in historical method and in the historical Jesus as a human being, about his teaching and ministry, not in his relationship with God. Theology "from above" is by contrast, she says, rooted in the authority of scripture and the identity and incarnation of Jesus as the Son of God.[54] She is not denying transcendence, but is rather arguing from the perspective of phenomenology, opening a side door on the question of religious language. Her objective is to counter the ideology she finds imposed by some feminist students upon the biblical texts that demonstrates the same kind of pride shown by males over the years. Her goal is thus to address a practical problem as it has played out in preaching: She strives to present an alternative and revisionist understanding of the faith that corrects self-promoting theologies and is grounded in history, tradition, and scripture.

Her accomplishment may be to allow the language of the faith to be employed anew by those who feel excluded by its history. Thus Bond is able to say that Jesus "acted like a son of God when he preached and enacted the reign of God"[55] without claiming who he is. She can say, "The story of his resurrection teaches us that his ministry of radical hospitality and his way of nonviolence are stronger than the powers of violence"[56] without saying that Jesus rose from the dead. She can affirm, "The presence of his ministry endures whenever new life emerges from crushing death"[57] without saying that Christ is risen and is present now. Her metaphorical theology rethinks christology in "salvaging" ways that she claims are able to split off the religious meanings of symbols from the metaphysical meanings and to avoid reducing a metaphor to its literal or idolatrous meaning.[58] Bond's purpose is positive; yet without being attentive to integrating what she calls theology from above, she may be open to misinterpretation. In Aristotle's substitution theory of language, metaphor can be tossed on the compost heap once the propositional content is obtained. Bond's notion that the metaphysical dimension of biblical metaphors can be discarded seems to be a version of Aristotle. What she proposes, if I understand her correctly, is like taking the skin from a banana and throwing out the fruit–you have something that looks like a banana but its substance is gone.

Evaluating Radical Postmodern Homiletics

If my radical postmodern colleagues are right, they represent a significant movement in homiletics. McClure is so confident of the radical postmodern ethic for homiletics that he says, "Even the New Homiletic has been left far behind, and there seems to be no looking back."[59] This can indeed be good news, for by this he means that preaching is now profoundly ethical, turning "toward its other(s) in such a way that preachers may re-encounter something of the nature of proclamation at its deepest levels."[60] This step offers many things to admire:

a. The radical postmodernists are trying to find ways to do theology that do not perpetuate the suffering done to particular groups in society.

b. They are attempting to include the stranger and outsider.

c. They are helping us to understand how that might be done.

If there is a problem, it may be in largely doing theology and homiletics by splitting off the Divine from the human, the above from the below.

The Need for a Practice- and Theory-Driven Homiletic

Radical postmodern homiletics is important because it engages homiletics in postmodern discourse theory and because it stands unequivocally for the marginalized and the ethical importance of their claims. This group is dedicating its work to rethinking doctrine and church life–a task we all must engage–and is willing to critique tradition. Contemporary homiletics does not do enough to help preachers improve the way they preach ethics and the work of the radical postmodernists needs to be heeded. In spite of recent attention, "preaching and ethics" remains an area needing much more attention. An area needing special attention is the practical working of ethical concerns into the sermon. Homiletics is a long way from providing practical homiletical guidance on these matters, and it is to homiletics in general that we now turn.

Four Homiletical Camps

A constant struggle for any of us in homiletics is to merge theory and praxis. Theory-driven homiletics is typically over-theorized or over-technical, rarely getting to the fundamental workings of sermons. Without explorations in new theologies and theories, homiletics can be in danger of becoming precisely what the radical postmodernists oppose: It can become insular and tradition-bound, no longer open to change. Those of us who are privileged to teach homiletics need also to struggle with an important fact: Homiletics belongs to practical theology for a reason.

Lucy Rose provides a largely worthy study of the range of homiletical options today, from old school to round table, yet she over-theorizes. She divides preaching into four camps:

1. traditional

2. kerygmatic

3. transformational

4. conversational

I have condensed the argument of her book into chart form.

TRADITIONAL		
PURPOSE AND CONTENT	**UNDERSTANDING OF LANGUAGE**	**SERMONS FORM(S)**
transmission of kerygma	objective	various forms
a central idea	can communicate clearly	central idea is foremost
information about God	can communicate truth	deductive
objective propositional truth	mediates God's Word	
persuasive discourse		

Problems with the Traditional for Rose

- The preacher is an authority figure who transmits truth to the congregation.
- The model is male (e.g., separation not connection).
- The sermon is the answer.
- Words correspond to objective reality.

KERYGMATIC

Purpose and Content	Understanding of Language	Sermons Form(s)
transmission of kerygma	mediates God's Word	various forms
an event of God speaking	communicates truth	one central idea is foremost
an act of revelation	reality is unchanging	text form may guide form
kerygmatic truth	language changes	
persuasive and eventful discourse	need for imagination	
a central idea		
preacher makes it an event		

Problems with the Kerygmatic for Rose

- Preacher remains an authority figure, though less than traditional.
- Solidarity between preacher and congregation is prevented.
- Every sermon cannot be an event.
- Emphasis is on the individual and personal encounter with God.
- Language is not capable of bearing an absolute unchanging kerygma.
- Translation of truth remains central, not interpretation of the Bible.

TRANSFORMATIONAL

Purpose and Content	Understanding of Language	Sermons Form(s)
Kerygma is not a fixed content	words shape consciousness	the story sermon
God makes it an event	words as events say and do	the inductive sermon
sermon as divine self-revelation	importance of metaphor	the narrative sermon
preacher under the Word	language reflects experience	plot
the Word transforms people	language shapes experience	enacts the message
congregation participates		generates an experience
hermeneutics over epistemology		
generative organic idea		

Problems with the Transformational for Rose

- Preacher and congregation are still separate.
- Preacher's experience may be presented as paradigmatic for all (Elisabeth Schüssler Fiorenza).
- All renderings of the text and experience are biased interpretations prone to fostering tyranny.
- Preaching should not assume that transformation is always needed.

CONVERSATIONAL (CROWD AROUND A TABLE)		
PURPOSE AND CONTENT	UNDERSTANDING OF LANGUAGE	SERMONS FORM(S)
release texts and interpretations	confessional	experiences of many
stimulates/refocuses conversations	reflects experience	interpretations
preacher and congregation are equal, connected	multivalent	convictions
interpretations (vs. revelation)	evocative	effect of *sermons*
a proposal (vs. Word)		open discourse (Q & A is permissible)
a wager (vs. kerygma)		a search for meaning
meaning (vs. truth)		inductive/narrative
story		story
uncertainty valued		multifocused (like a play)
control: conversation & God		open-ended
generates many meanings, wagers		ecclesial not clerical style
scripture a record of experiences		

Critique of Rose

The people Rose names in each camp do not, in fact, display all the attributes she assigns to them on sermonic purpose, content, language, and shape.[61] Eugene Lowry wants to save Rose from her own conversational camp (i.e., radical postmodern) by dissolving it into the transformational.[62] I question whether the kergymatic and the transformational can be helpfully separated. The transformational is transformational not because it evokes experience or changes consciousness. If it were only this, it would just be bad or manipulative preaching. It is transformational because it preaches the central story of Christ (i.e., the kerygma) into experience in such a way that Christ is found there. Perhaps only three categories are workable beyond the category of just plain bad:

1. traditional preaching (ideational, expository preaching, often kerygmatic)
2. New Homiletic preaching (kerygmatic, transformative, postmodern, conversational)
3. radical postmodern preaching (mostly anthropocentric, ethics-centered, conversational, collaborative, roundtable, often apparently non-kerygmatic, occasionally post-Christian)[63]

Problems of Being Interdisciplinary

NOT DOING JUSTICE TO A DISCIPLINE

Homiletics is appropriately interdisciplinary, yet four problems typically emerge in this regard. First, in spanning two disciplines, we can fail to do justice to one or the other. The work of an ethicist in homiletics is different in nature from the work of an ethicist in theology, though both move from theology and faith to behavior. Theological ethics, at least in one understanding, tries to establish a coherent pattern of ethics and ethical decision-making and is particularly important in these postmodern times, when moral standards are relativized. What we may call homiletical ethics by contrast moves (a) between theological ethics and the pulpit, and (b) from theological reflection on a particular biblical text to ethical behavior in a particular congregation and community, or vice versa. Homiletical ethics, as I conceive it, tries to establish ways to strengthen the ethical reflection of preachers and to determine what might guide them best to accomplish the sermon's ethical goals.

IGNORING HOMILETICS

Second, homileticians are notorious for ignoring their own discipline and favoring others. Christine Smith in *Risking the Terror* and John McClure in *Other-Wise Preaching* both strike out in directions that largely ignore homiletics, and that may be necessary from time to time. Given the lack of adequate attention to ethics in homiletics, they may deserve commendation. Still, one could caution that homileticians in general need to serve their own discipline first and foremost.

PLACING DERIVED THEORY OVER PRACTICE

Third, homiletics is prone to putting theory devised from other disciplines ahead of practice, in two ways:

1. Giving short shrift to practical matters. When theory is imported, it needs to be rendered in a manner that is both more practical and accessible than in the original source. Some people might argue that as homileticians we can write for other homileticians and be justified in staying theoretical. Again, one need not have a hard and fast rule, yet I argue that the other theological disciplines exist to serve that function. Further, questions of sermon excellence and conformity to the gospel need at least as much attention as other matters. No one set of standards will satisfy the need, but some sets of standards ought to be a project of the discipline as a whole. Preachers depend on homiletics to think through what it is they do and to help them to do it with greater economy, skill, and insight. To meet this need, the practice of preaching must generate new theory, and the theory of preaching must generate new practice, the two always being linked and integrated.

2. Ignoring actual sermons. Homiletics needs to arise out of and lead to actual sermons—and not just adequate sermons but excellent ones—and needs to be guided by excellent sermons in the past or present. Homiletical writing exists to help preachers know how to proceed in preaching a biblical text and may demonstrate the authors' own struggles. In fact, the pulpit must not only be in view but ought to be seen to be in view. One could argue that otherwise, our writing is in danger of taking preachers only to the doorstep of homiletics.

UNCRITICAL ADOPTION OF IDEOLOGY

Fourth, all disciplines are dependent upon other disciplines, yet homiletics is particularly so. It is therefore arguably more in danger of adopting uncritically whatever ideology comes along, be it historical-critical method, language theory, splitting the Divine from the human, the reduction of God to a scientific worldview, the privileging of homiletical theory over practice or practice over theory, or whatever. For example, even justice can become an ideology without appropriate scrutiny. Not everyone who is marginalized by history or society is a victim: Some are oppressors, pimps, drug pushers, pedophiles, sociopaths. Some mechanism for distinguishing among the claims of the marginalized is needed. Moreover, nearly everyone in our era feels like a victim, whether this perceived victimization is real or not, be it: economic (e.g., insufficient earnings); physical (e.g., trouble with health care); social (e.g., overwork); political (e.g., underrepresented); environmental (e.g., the effects of pollution), or whatever. Also, as Charles Bartow says, "while God indeed may be on the side of the poor and marginalized, God may not be there always *as the poor themselves suppose* (the definition of *holy* justice finally remains with the Word of God…)"[64] Further, what happens to those individuals in our culture and churches who we might determine are not marginalized? Is the gospel for them?

An Alternative Ethic for Homiletics

I will now attempt to make some constructive recommendations for homiletics as a whole. These recommendations seek to build on an ethic of homiletics as devised by the radical group, yet there is room here only to sketch briefly what might well be a project for the discipline as a whole. Some of its features are already demonstrated, at least in part, by many of the people we have studied in chapter 8.

1. How we do homiletics is an ethical matter, not just in terms of what sources are used and what issues are discussed, but also in a commitment to serve the preaching needs of the church, to preach the gospel, and to build up the community of faith. Homiletics thus seeks to facilitate an encounter with the triune God and to foster loving action on the part of communities that are dedicated to moral responsibility and social justice. Were homiletical theory to lose sight of this goal, it could be interpreted to be remote from the practice of those it seeks to serve. At that point there would be nothing to distinguish homiletics from the other disciplines to which it necessarily relates–its homiletical reason for being would be gone.

2. Second, homiletics must be realistic in its interpretation of the church. Lenora Tubbs Tisdale recommends that theology in a sermon be "'seriously imaginable' within a local community of faith,"[65] and something of that is a useful guide for homiletics as well. The radical postmodernists are concerned about preaching–that is why they are teaching it. Bond does not advocate that preachers proclaim at a funeral, "Jesus is a good metaphor of our hope," or at Easter, "It is as though Jesus rose from the dead." But a student could be excused for reading her that way. Similarly Webb, who is repeatedly dealing with practical homiletical matters, might be mistaken to recommend saying, "If it helps, we can think of Jesus as risen from the dead." McClure similarly could easily be misread to be so other-focused that the needs of those present are overlooked, yet in his *Roundtable Pulpit* he makes clear that the other, at the deepest level, is every human being.[66] Of course, anyone can be misread. Caution is simply needed to be clear, not least on practical concerns.

3. Because homiletics serves preaching, homiletics is conservative in relation to tradition and radical in terms of the gospel. Homiletics generally follows the practice of the church and leads it only when it has an insight or innovation that demonstrates obvious benefit. Homiletics needs to be theory- and practice-driven, the practice of preaching generating new theory and the theory of preaching generating new practice. The two should keep each other in check. Tradition needs to be critiqued, and doctrine must be rethought for every generation. This must be done without discarding many of the ways our ancestors read scripture, for were that to happen, what is to stop racists, bigots, warmongers, and others from adopting the same tactics to justify their practices? The Bible becomes scripture because it has the capacity to reveal God's actions and human identity in history and in the present. In light of this it may be seen (a) to tell the stories of people who prevailed against injustice, and (b) to distance the reader from his or her assumed identity.[67] Both the Divine and the human perspective need to be considered and both have something to teach.

4. Finally, ethics is stronger in the presence of proclamation of the gospel because people are cast on God's resources. Ethics becomes radical because it is transformational and empowered. So we come then to where we started. Preaching can be ethics; but when that is all that preaching is, it is simply teaching. Then we as listeners emerge with understanding. At the end of proclamation, however, where ethics plays a significant role, we may emerge with a sense of being redeemed and empowered by God to perform the moral and social duties we are called to do as Christ's disciples. And in saying that we begin to glimpse the new creation Christ is laboring to achieve. I propose the following guidelines almost by way of summary:

Guidelines for Ethical Homiletics

Homiletics is done in an ethical manner.

Homiletics exists to serve the preaching needs of the church.

Homiletics seeks to facilitate an encounter with the triune God.

Homiletics is rooted in the Bible and its critical heritage.

Homiletics encourages a theological reading of the Bible.

Homiletics seeks to foster loving action on the part of communities dedicated to moral responsibility and social justice.

Homiletics arises out of and leads to actual sermons.

Homiletics is devoted to helping preachers think through what it is they do.

Homiletics is devoted to helping preachers to prepare sermons with greater economy, skill, and insight.

Homiletics is devoted to preaching excellence and to determining standards of that excellence.

Homiletics engages homiletical literature.

Homiletics is interdisciplinary, mediating between other disciplines and preaching practice.

Homiletics is theory- and practice-driven. The practice of preaching generates new theory, and the theory of preaching generates new practice; the two are always linked.

Homiletics is realistic in its interpretation of the church.

Homiletics is conservative in terms of its innovation and radical in terms of the gospel.

Practical Ethics

Keeping in mind that homiletics must be practical, we conclude with explicit direction for sermons. Sermons in previous ages, even from people who were social activists like John Wesley,[68] contained surprisingly little comment on ethical issues. It is as though his social ministry was lived, not preached, and people so knew of the Methodist emphasis on education and social welfare that he did not need to preach it, but to inspire it. It was so present in people's thoughts and weekly lives that the mechanics of it did not need to be discussed in the sermon. On the other hand, much preaching on individual and corporate behavior in the present day is moralistic: The gospel message turns into do's and don'ts that have an anthropocentric flavor and little mention of whether God cares about the ethical issues mentioned, or empowers change.

From the perspective of the trouble/grace school of homiletics, a substantial treatment of ethical demand and a substantial focus on grace and faith almost seem to be at odds. Some reasons for this are clear:

1. In the trouble/grace school, a preacher takes a good deal of sermon time to develop effectively the trouble from a biblical text for today. Ideally this will be done from a theological perspective, matters of God and faith will be plainly in view, and this portion of the sermon will not be reduced to sociology or ideology.[69]

2. It takes just as long in a sermon to develop a dependence upon God.

3. Ethical analysis demands more sermon time than many preachers have and more careful nuance of thought than many congregations want to receive or are able to follow.

4. Major discussion of a troubling ethical issue in a biblical sermon can easily be heard in itself as trouble and has the potential to divide the congregation.

5. Sermons ought not to sound like essays and lectures of the sort that ethical analysis easily becomes.

6. In fact, among the various other ethical dimensions of preaching (establishing norms, values, standards, and principles; clarifying faith; appealing to authority; developing moral character), the sermon is least suited to ethical analysis.[70]

An ethical direction for the sermon normally will arise from the biblical text itself. The moral sense of our preaching ancestors[71] provided practical advice that enabled people to live their lives and was therefore a form of wisdom literature. From our own perspective, many of the meanings they found were not authentic morals arising out of the texts at hand, yet more responsible treatment of the moral sense of scripture is possible. When preachers speak of some behavioral outcome of a sermon, they may be demonstrating it, for scripture naturally leads to some change in behavior. The Reformed tradition affirms only one sense of scripture, the literal sense, yet we have continued to use an ancient moral sense of scripture without ever acknowledging it.

Every time a biblical sermon suggests an action for the congregation to follow, a moral sense or ethic is being invoked. Sometimes this moral action is directed by the direct literal reading of the text. More frequently, it requires looking for a moral even when one is not obvious, ensuring that it is in fact legitimate and not moralizing. Sometimes the moral arises out of a principle like loving one's neighbor. Sometimes it arises out of imitating a practice observed in a text, for instance the faithfulness of the friends in the healing of the paralytic (Mk. 2:1–12).

Sometimes it arises out of understanding that God's actions have direct implication for our behavior, for instance God's generosity toward us requires our generosity toward others. Often the moral is to one side of a text; that is, it is not in the primary direction of focus.

An example of the last point may be found in many of the difficult texts involving Jesus. As I have argued elsewhere:

Still, even in such [difficult] texts a moral can be discerned, though not one involving direct imitation of Christ: Christ overturning the tables in the Temple (Mark 11:15-19) speaks of the need to avoid defiling the holy; his condemnation of the fig tree out of season (Mark 11:12-14) speaks to the urgent need for change now; his command to tear out your own eye rather than sin (Matthew 5:29) speaks against judging others; his not bringing peace but a sword (Matthew 10:34-36) speaks of full commitment to Christ; his rebuke of his mother (John 2:4) speaks against assuming that our agendas are God's; his delaying two days to respond to Lazarus's illness (John 11:6) speaks to the same thing; his condemnation of all the scribes and Pharisees (Matthew 23) speaks against presuming self-righteousness; his commending of the dishonest Steward (Luke 16:1-7) speaks of the need for Christ's followers to be shrewd ; and his narrative treatment of the elder son (Luke 15:11-32) is a caution against works righteousness.[72]

Preachers who do not develop a God sense of scripture, as is the tendency of the radical postmodernists, actually deprive themselves of a legitimate moral arising from the text. The action that God performs in or behind a biblical text in itself holds clues for human behavior. Or moving in the other theological direction, Luther helped us to see that the moral sense leads back to God, for the very action required of humanity is the action that God empowers. In other words, ethics properly construed is not just a burden–it is an empowered opportunity.

We have drawn to the end of our study of the relationship of preaching and homiletical theory. We still have many books left to discuss, many that would have been good to be able to include here or to afford more than passing reference. Nonetheless, we have journeyed a considerable distance through homiletical terrain having to do with the Bible, theology, and practical theology. Although our study is less than comprehensive, we have seen much of the richness of homiletics today. Our purpose from the outset has been to identify significant movements in homiletical theory and to assess their usefulness for preaching. Homiletics is old; yet as an academic discipline with its own considerable body of literature, it is also relatively new and exciting.

Among the developments we have discussed are the following. We have seen the change in theme sentence from a static, propositional statement to a double-barreled dynamic entity that spans the gap between then and now. It is concerned with both saying and doing what the biblical text says and does, or with what God in the biblical text says and does. We have seen a reawakening of homiletical interest in exegesis for preaching, not as the objective science it once was thought to be, but as an exercise that now must be not only historical but also literary, theological, and contextual or homiletical. We have argued that the biblical text has become more fluid as preachers perceive the need for intertextual links in preaching; moreover, the boundaries separating exegesis, hermeneutics, and homiletics are more fluid, even as the activities they represent have become more playful and creative. New commentaries are being written to help preachers deal specifically with preaching biblical books that pose unusual problems for preachers. We have traced a growth in understandings of the interrelation between sermon form and content in homiletical theory, and with it appreciation for the eventful, performative, and transformative nature of the Word.

We have also examined the growth of two current homiletical schools, including the radical postmodern. For the most part, trouble and grace had not been identified as a school in homiletics. In one of its expressions, it has roots in Lutheran theology, though it was never confined there, and in the last quarter century has spread inter-denominationally and now has representatives from widely diverse traditions, from evangelical Protestant to Roman Catholic. The other expression of trouble/grace is African American, representing various traditions rooted in transplantation, suffering, and oppression. Although these two branches seem widely different, from the perspective of theological structure, they share much in common and are closely allied. They need to be in dialogue as one school. This dialogue would allow the former to strengthen its homiletical practice, and the latter to strengthen its homiletical theory.

In the process of our study we have also presented a vision of preaching in the future and unearthed some challenges for homiletics as a discipline. Among these we may highlight seven:

1. Excellence needs to become the stated goal of homiletics to replace adequacy as a norm. This may involve: conceiving of homiletics primarily as a theological venture that needs to speak directly of God; responsible homiletical scholarship that takes account of what others in the discipline have said; and consistent linking theory and practice.

2. Homiletical writers of biblical commentaries may improve their offerings by stating clear theoretical goals concerning homiletics and by articulating the distinctive nature of what they hope to achieve.

3. As reader response and other ways of reading the Bible make increasing inroads, often opening new preaching possibilities in difficult texts, attention must be given as to the ways in which these texts are authoritative for the church and what safeguards may be devised for biblical interpretation and preaching.

4. Preachers need encouragement to shift their emphasis to preaching the gospel and away from preaching pericopes *per se.* Pericopes provide essential, irreplaceable windows to the gospel, and sometimes contain a fulsome expression of it, but rarely fully embody it themselves if treated in isolation from the rest of the biblical story.

5. New theoretical understandings of the idea of biblical text in the sermon await to be conceived, given (a) that the text is more properly the particular passage *along with* its intertextual connections to the entire gospel message, and (b) that what the sermon represents as the biblical text is an improvisation of it, or an adaptation, or a pseudo-text (Gerhard von Rad spoke of an actualization). Said another way, we need to clarify two impulses that overlap and interpenetrate in preaching, yet may also have distinctive features, representation, and interpretation of the biblical text.

6. Urgent attention is needed to help preachers to preach the gospel *and* ethics, instead of one or the other, and to provide guidance toward boldness in this regard. A large part of the challenge is to include global perspectives absent from the majority of North American preaching, for example, caring for the world's poor and sick, for God's creation, and working for peace and justice.

7. Finally, a paradigm shift is needed in homiletics as a whole to return God to the center of scripture. The Bible may be read using many rich and rewarding lenses, but the most important lens for the church is the Bible as revelation, and it involves looking for who God is and the roles we humans are meant to fill in God's great plan.

In these pages we have discovered within homiletics a care for the church and its preaching that bodes well for the future. Much fine work is being done. If homiletics continues to conceive of itself as having one foot in the church and the other in the academy and if homileticians continue to conceive of their teaching as a vocation to

NOTES

Chapter 1: Biblical Preaching

[1]Stephen Farris, *Preaching That Matters: The Bible and Our Lives* (Louisville: Westminster John Knox Press, 1998), 7.

[2]Johann Michael Reu, *Homiletics,* trans. Albert Steinhaeuser (Grand Rapids: Baker Book House, 1967 [1922]), 437.

[3]H. Grady Davis, *Design for Preaching* (Philadelphia: Fortress Press, 1958), 43–44.

[4]Haddon W. Robinson, *Biblical Preaching: The Development and Delivery of Expository Messages* (Grand Rapids: Baker Academic, 2d ed., 2001 [1980]), 41; see 33–50.

[5]Ibid., 45.

[6]Ibid., 40. Keith Willhite and Scott M. Gibson, eds., *The Big Idea of Biblical Preaching* (Grand Rapids: Baker Books, 1998) offers helpful commentary on Robinson's method. Willhite cites Timothy Warren, who amplified Robinson's homiletic. Warren envisioned a three-step process of exegesis, theology, and homiletics, each of which determines a subject (what is it about?) and a complement (what is it saying about the subject?). The exegetical idea is in the language of the text. The theological idea is in more timeless language. And the homiletical idea, again composed of a subject (what am I talking about?) and a complement (what exactly am I saying about what I am talking about?), is in contemporary language and phrased as an imperative. Keith Willhite notes how an intermediate theological step (again, subject + complement) strengthens the process. For example, the exegetical idea might be, "The reason Paul commanded the Ephesian believers to praise God was because God has guaranteed their future inheritance through the ministry of the Holy Spirit." The theological idea might be, "Praise to God is the proper response for a guaranteed inheritance." And the homiletical idea around which the sermon is composed might be, "Praise God because of the inheritance that the Holy Spirit guarantees you" (17–18). See Timothy S. Warren, "A Paradigm for Preachers," *Bibliotheca Sacra* 148 (October-December 1991): 463–86.

[7]Fred B. Craddock, *Preaching* (Nashville: Abingdon Press, 1985), 122.

[8]Thomas G. Long, *The Witness of Preaching* (Louisville: Westminster/John Knox Press, 1989), 86.

[9]Craddock, *Preaching,* 122. See Thomas G. Long, *Preaching and the Literary Forms of the Bible* (Philadelphia: Fortress Press, 1989), esp. 11–22.

[10]Eugene H. Peterson, *The Message: The Bible in Contemporary Language* (Colorado Springs: NavPress, 2002).

[11]Long, *Witness of Preaching,* 86.

[12]The origin of Craddock's two questions may be traced to his *As One Without Authority* (Nashville: Abingdon Press, 1979 [1971]), where he has preachers ask of texts, "Who is saying what to whom and for what reasons?"(137).

[13]Long, *Witness of Preaching,* 84. He cited appreciatively David Kelsey's words, "Part of what it means to call a text 'Christian scripture' is that *it functions to shape persons' identities so decisively as to transform them...when it is used in the context of the common life of Christian community.*" See David H. Kelsey, *The Use of Scripture in Recent Theology* (Philadelphia: Fortress Press, 1975), 91.

[14]Paul Scott Wilson, *God Sense: Reading the Bible for Preaching* (Nashville: Abingdon Press, 2001).

[15]"What is that God who created the world...doing, according to the words of this biblical passage?" Elizabeth Achtemeier, *The Old Testament and the Proclamation of the Gospel* (Philadelphia: The Westminster Press, 1973) 37.

[16]Ibid., esp. 9–20, 65–68, 85–90.

[17]Paul Scott Wilson, *Imagination of the Heart: New Understandings in Preaching* (Nashville: Abingdon Press, 1988), 86–90, 112–127; and *The Practice of Preaching* (Nashville: Abingdon Press, 1995), esp. 164–71.

[18]Foster R. McCurley follows a similar "text sentence" and "sermon sentence" in his *Wrestling with the Word: Preaching from the Hebrew Bible* (Valley Forge, Pa.: Trinity Press International, 1996), 53–54.

[19]Bryan Chapell, *Christ-Centered Preaching: Redeeming the Expository Sermon* (Grand Rapids: Baker Books, 1994), 42.

[20]Ibid., 266.

[21]Harold T. Bryson and James C. Taylor, *Building Sermons to Meet People's Needs* (Nashville: Broadman Press, 1980), 52–68.

[22]John Killinger, *Fundamentals of Preaching* (Philadelphia: Fortress Press, 1985), 44–50, esp. 49.

[23]James Cox, *Preaching: A Comprehensive Approach to the Design and Delivery of Sermons* (San Francisco: Harper and Row, 1985), 77–88, 89–115.

[24]Henry Mitchell, *Celebration and Experience in Preaching* (Nashville: Abingdon Press, 1990), 52.

[25]Stephen Farris, *Preaching That Matters,* 71–72.

[26]Jana Childers, "A Shameless Path," in *Birthing the Sermon: Women Preachers on the Creative Process,* ed. Jana Childers (St. Louis: Chalice Press, 2001), 43.

[27]Alyce M. McKenzie, *Preaching Proverbs: Wisdom for the Pulpit* (Louisville: Westminster John Knox Press, 1996), 19.

[28]Alyce M. McKenzie, *Preaching Biblical Wisdom in a Self-Help Society* (Nashville: Abingdon Press, 2002).

[29]Sidney Greidanus, *The Modern Preacher and the Ancient Text* (Grand Rapids: William B. Eerdmans Publishing Company, 1988), 157–84.

[30]David Buttrick, *Homiletic: Moves and Structures* (Philadelphia: Fortress Press, 1987), 29.

[31]Ibid., 41.

[32]Ibid., 25.

[33]Ibid., 37.

[34]Ibid., 28.

[35]Ibid., 51.

[36]Ibid., 41.

[37]Ibid., 18.

[38]Richard L. Eslinger, *Narrative and Imagination: Preaching the Worlds That Shape Us* (Minneapolis: Fortress Press, 1995), 9.

[39]Ibid., 36.

[40]Ibid., 28–29.

[41]Eugene L. Lowry, *The Sermon: Dancing the Edge of Mystery* (Nashville: Abingdon Press, 1997), 108.

[42]Ibid., 107.

[43]Ibid.

[44]Ibid., 117.

[45]Ibid., 52.

[46]John S. McClure, *The Roundtable Pulpit* (Nashville: Abingdon Press, 1995); *The Four Codes of Preaching: Rhetorical Strategies* (Minneapolis: Fortress Press, 1991).

[47]Lucy Atkinson Rose, *Sharing the Word: Preaching in the Roundtable Church* (Louisville: Westminster John Knox Press, 1997), 104.

[48]Ibid., 117.

[49]Ibid., 105.

[50]Ibid., 130.

[51]Richard Eslinger argues for a difference between a theme sentence approach and Buttrick's moves: "from Buttrick's side, the structure and dynamic of the sermon is provided through a plotting of these moves with an eye toward intention. The unity of the sermon, Buttrick would insist, is a byproduct of a carefully shaped sequence of moves intending to form in the consciousness of the listeners." Richard L. Eslinger, *The Web of Preaching: New Options in Homiletic Method* (Nashville: Abingdon Press, 2002), 97.

[52]An excellent example of what it means to preach an image is Tom Troeger's sermon "Rising River," in his *Ten Strategies for Preaching in a Multi-Media Culture* (Nashville: Abingdon Press, 1996), 68–77.

Chapter 2: Exegesis for Preaching

[1]Numbers may not mean much, yet the Society for Biblical Literature (SBL), the academic association of biblical scholars, has around 12,000 members worldwide, while the three homiletics associations, the Academy of Homiletics, Societas Homiletica, and the Evangelical Homiletics Society probably have a combined total of around 750. (Many homileticians belong to more than one and also to the SBL.)

[2]Otto Kaiser and Werner G. Kümmel, *Exegetical Method: A Student's Handbook,* trans. E. V. N. Goetchius (New York: Seabury Press, 1967 [Munchen: Chr. Kaiser Verlag, 1963]).

[3]Ibid., 36.

[4]Ibid., 36–37.

[5]Here I provide my own amalgamated rendering of Kümmel's method, found on pages 37–70, altering his order slightly for the purposes of clarity here.

[6]Richard B. Hays, "Exegesis," in William Willimon and Richard Lischer, eds., *Concise Encyclopedia of Preaching* (Louisville: Westminster John Knox Press, 1995), 122–28, esp. 122.

[7]Notably, J. H. Hayes and C. R. Holladay, *Biblical Exegesis: A Beginner's Handbook* (Louisville: Westminster/John Knox Press, 1987 [1982]); Gordon D. Fee, *New Testament Exegesis: A Handbook for Students and Pastors* (Louisville: Westminster John Knox Press, 2002 [1993]); G. R. Osborne, *The Hermeneutical Spiral: A Comprehensive Introduction to Biblical Interpretation* (Downers Grove, Ill.: InterVarsity Press, 1991); Christopher Tuckett, *Reading the New Testament: Methods of Interpretation* (Minneapolis: Fortress Press, 1993); Hans Odil Steck, *Old Testament Exegesis,* trans. James D. Nogalski (Atlanta: Scholars Press, 1995); *Biblical Hermeneutics: A Comprehensive Introduction to Interpreting Scripture* (Nashville: Broadman and Holman, 1996); *A Guide to Old Testament Theology and Exegesis,* ed. Willem A. VanGemeren (Grand Rapids: Zondervan, 1999 [1997]); *Interpreting the New Testament,* ed. David Alan Black and David S. Dockery (Nashville: Broadman and Holman, 2001). Several works devoted to specific areas of exegesis have appeared including *Old Testament Form Criticism,* ed. John H. Hayes (San Antonio: Trinity University Press, 1974); *Beyond Form Criticism,* ed. Paul R. House (Winona Lake, Ind.: Eisenbrauns, 1992); *The Changing Face of Form Criticism for the Twenty-First Century,* ed. Marvin A. Sweeney and Ehud Ben Zvi (Grand Rapids: Eerdmans, 2003); and Fortress Press's Guides to Biblical Scholarship series.

[8]Johann Michael Reu, *Homiletics* (Grand Rapids: Baker Book House, 1967 [1922]), 338–61, 527–604.

[9]Leander E. Keck, *The Bible in the Pulpit: The Renewal of Biblical Preaching* (Nashville: Abingdon Press, 1978).

[10]Ibid., 115.

[11]Ibid.

[12]Among the numerous important volumes that put renewed focus on the Bible are (in chronological order): William D. Thompson, *Preaching Biblically: Exegesis and Interpretation,* Abingdon Preacher's Library (Nashville: Abingdon Press, 1981); James W. Cox, ed., *Biblical Preaching, An Expositor's Treasury* (Philadelphia: The Westminster Press, 1983); Richard White, *Biblical Preaching: How to Find and Remove the Barriers* (St. Louis: CBP Press, 1988); Raymond Bailey, contributing ed., *Hermeneutics for Preaching: Approaches to Contemporary Interpretations of Scripture* (Nashville: Broadman Press, 1992).

[13]Don M. Wardlaw, ed., *Preaching Biblically: Creating Sermons in the Shape of Scripture* (Philadelphia: The Westminster Press, 1983).

[14]Ronald J. Allen, *Contemporary Bibilical Interpretation for Preaching* (Valley Forge, Pa.: Judson Press, 1984).

¹⁵In 1991 with Clark M. Williamson, Allen wrote a volume containing excellent chapters on process hermeneutics and biblical interpretation. Their process hermeneutics could be called postmodern today: They uphold a theocentric norm, intellectual credibility, and moral plausibility as guides for interpretation, as well as a higher goal than truth. Ronald J. Allen and Clark M. Williamson, *A Credible and Timely Word: Process Theology and Preaching* (St. Louis: Chalice Press, 1991), 71–129, esp. 71–83.

¹⁶Thomas G. Long, *Preaching and the Literary Forms of the Bible* (Philadelphia: Fortress Press, 1989), see p. 13.

¹⁷Ibid., 33.

¹⁸David L. Bartlett, *Between the Bible and the Church: New Methods for Biblical Preaching* (Nashville: Abingdon Press, 1999).

¹⁹Ibid., 16–17.

²⁰Ibid., 40.

²¹Ibid., 29.

²²Ibid., 24.

²³ Paul Scott Wilson, *God Sense: Reading the Bible for Preaching* (Nashville: Abingdon Press, 2001).

²⁴See Thomas G. Long, *The Witness of Preaching* (Louisville: Westminster/John Knox Press, 1989); Stephen Farris, *Preaching That Matters: The Bible and Our Lives* (Louisville: Westminster John Knox Press, 1998); Ronald J. Allen, *Preaching: An Essential Guide* (Nashville: Abingdon Press, 2002); Paul Scott Wilson, *The Practice of Preaching* (Nashville: Abingdon Press, 1995).

²⁵Here I am thinking for instance of Bryan Chapell, *Christ-Centered Preaching: Redeeming the Expository Sermon* (Grand Rapids: Baker Books, 1994); *Handbook of Contemporary Preaching*, ed. Michael Duduit (Nashville: Broadman Press, 1992); Sidney Greidanus, *The Modern Preacher and the Ancient Text* (Grand Rapids: William B. Eerdmans, 1988); Haddon W. Robinson, *Biblical Preaching: The Development and Delivery of Expository Messages* (Grand Rapids: Baker Academic, 2d ed., 2001 [1980]); John Stott, *I Believe in Preaching* (London, Sydney, Auckland: Hodden & Stoughton, 1983).

²⁶Karl Barth was a leader in this direction that finds continuing expression, for instance, in the work of Walter Bruggemann, Brevard Childs, and others.

²⁷Fred B. Craddock, *Preaching* (Nashville: Abingdon Press, 1985), 106.

²⁸Ibid., 105–17.

²⁹Ibid., 117–20.

³⁰Ibid., 119.

³¹Ibid., 121–24, esp. 122.

³²Bartlett, *Between the Bible and the Church*, 24.

³³Long, *Witness*, 67–68.

³⁴Ibid., 66–72.

³⁵Paul Scott Wilson, *Imagination of the Heart: New Understandings in Preaching* (Nashville: Abingdon Press, 2001), 58.

³⁶Charles L. Rice, *Imagination and Interpretation* (Philadelphia: Fortress Press, 1970).

³⁷Walter Brueggemann, *The Prophetic Imagination* (Minneapolis: Fortress Press, 1978); and *Finally Comes the Poet* (Minneapolis: Fortress Press, 1989); Thomas H. Troeger, *Creating Fresh Images for Preaching* (Valley Forge, Pa.: Judson Press, 1982) and *Imagining the Sermon* (Nashville: Abingdon Press, 1990); William J. Bausch, *Storytelling: Imagination and Faith* (Mystic, Conn.: Twenty-Third Publications, 1984); Paul Scott Wilson, *Imagination of the Heart*, in which pastor and prophet are linked; see also the discussion of ethical imagination in my "Beyond Narrative: Imagination in the Sermon," in *Listening to the Word: Studies in Honor of Fred B. Craddock*, ed. Gail R. O'Day and Thomas G. Long (Nashville: Abingdon Press, 1993), 131–46; Eduard R. Riegert, *Imaginative Shock: Preaching and Metaphor* (Burlington, Ontario: Trinity Press, 1990); James A. Wallace, *Imaginal Preaching: An Archetypal Perspective* (New York: Paulist Press, 1995); Richard L. Eslinger, *Narrative and Imagination: Preaching the Worlds That Shape Us* (Minneapolis: Fortress Press, 1995); Ellen F. Davis, *Imagination Shaped: Old Testament Preaching in the Anglican Tradition* (Valley Forge, Pa.: Trinity Press, 1995); Mary Catherine Hilkert,

Naming Grace: Preaching and the Sacramental Imagination (New York: The Continuum Publishing Company, 1997).

[38]Jana Childers, ed., *Birthing the Sermon: Women Preachers on the Creative Process* (St. Louis: Chalice Press, 2001); Cleophus J. LaRue, ed., *Power in the Pulpit: How America's Most Effective Black Preachers Prepare Their Sermons* (Louisville: Westminster John Knox Press, 2002).

[39]Karen Stokes, "Inbreeding," in Childers, *Birthing*, 146–52, esp. 151.

[40]One of these is excellent for being concise, Mark Barger Elliott, *Creative Styles of Preaching* (Louisville: Westminster John Knox Press, 2000); Ronald Allen's offering provides the most range, *Patterns of Preaching: A Sermon Sampler* (St. Louis: Chalice Press, 1998). Note also: Eduard R. Riegert, *Hear Then a Story: Plot Possibilities for Story Sermons* (Waterloo, Ontario: Waterloo Lutheran Seminary, 2000); Richard L. Eslinger, *The Web of Preaching: New Options in Homiletic Method* (Nashville: Abingdon Press, 2002), esp. 46–287. Two authors have been willing to risk their own creative sermon designs: Eugene L. Lowry, *How to Preach a Parable: Designs for Narrative Sermons* (Nashville: Abingdon Press, 1991); Thomas Troeger, *The Parable of Ten Preachers* (Nashville: Abingdon Press, 1994) and *Ten Strategies for Preaching in a Multi-Media Culture* (Nashville: Abingdon Press, 1996).

[41]Don M. Wardlaw articulated a relational approach to the Bible in his, "Preaching as the Interface of Two Social Worlds," in *Preaching as a Social Act: Theology and Practice,* ed. Arthur Van Seters (Nashville: Abingdon Press, 1988), 55–94, esp. 58–63; see also Walter Brueggemann's understandings of socially nested interests past and present in his, "The Social Nature of the Biblical Text for Preaching," in Van Seters, 127–66.

[42]Stephen Farris, *Preaching That Matters: The Bible and Our Lives* (Louisville: Westminster John Knox Press, 1998), 51–74.

[43]Ibid., 73.

[44]Ibid., 74.

[45]Ibid., 71.

[46]Ibid., 74.

[47]Ibid., 31–32.

[48]Ibid., 36–38.

[49]Wilson, *God Sense,* 69–71; see also Wilson, *Practice,* 133–36; 138–39.

[50]Hayes and Holladay, *Biblical Exegesis,* 123.

[51]Walter Brueggemann, *Genesis,* Interpretation: A Bible Commentary for Teaching and Preaching (Atlanta: John Knox Press, 1982), vii.

[52]See, for instance, Paul Scott Wilson, *The Four Pages of the Sermon: A Guide to Biblical Preaching* (Nashville: Abingdon Press, 1999).

[53]Don M. Wardlaw, ed., *Preaching Biblically: Creating Sermons in the Shape of Scripture* (Philadelphia: The Westminster Press, 1983). I am grateful for a conversation with Art Van Seters on the significance of this book.

[54]Richard White spoke of the creativity of the sermon being found in the biblical text in his, "The Authority of the Text Versus Creative Interpretation," *Papers of the Academy of Homiletics,* December 7–9, 1978, Princeton, N.J.

[55]Cited from the back cover of Wardlaw, *Preaching Biblically.*

[56]Thomas G. Long, *Preaching and the Literary Forms of the Bible* (Philadelphia: Fortress Press, 1989), 13.

[57]Ibid., 33.

[58]Ibid., 47.

[59]Ibid., 22–126.

[60]Mike Graves, *The Sermon as Symphony: Preaching the Literary Forms of the New Testament* (Valley Forge, Pa.: Judson Press, 1997). See also David L. Bartlett, "Texts Shaping Sermons," in *Listening to the Word: Studies in Honor of Fred B. Craddock,* ed. Gail R. O'Day & Thomas G. Long (Nashville: Abingdon Press, 1993), 147–63.

[61]Bruce E. Shields, *From the Housetops: Preaching in the Early Church and Today* (St. Louis: Chalice Press, 2000), 159–60.

Chapter 3: Homileticians and the Bible

[1]Today some published commentaries provide little help connecting the text to the contemporary setting and are written for colleagues in academic departments rather than preachers. One can no longer assume that the biblical commentator has the interests of the church foremost, as opposed to the interests of history, archeology, comparative religion, or some other discipline. Because many biblical scholars are uncomfortable in speaking of revelation, it is now often helpful to distinguish between the Bible and scripture to avoid confusion when referring to God's Word as revelation. Still, many essential things are said about the Bible from these perspectives that assist proclamation, but some scholars even regard the recent appearance of biblical-homiletical volumes cynically, seeing them as a sign of declining academic standards in our time. For this problem in biblical studies, see Carl E. Bratten and Robert W. Jenson, eds., *Reclaiming the Bible for the Church* (Grand Rapids: William B. Eerdmans Publishing Company, 1995).

[2]Leander Keck, senior ed., *The New Interpreter's Bible,* 12 vols. (Nashville: Abingdon Press, 1994–98); *Interpretation: A Bible Commentary for Teaching and Preaching* series from John Knox Press; compare the *Preaching Classic Texts* series from Chalice Press and the "multimedia" approach of the *Smyth and Helwys Bible Commentary* complete with CD rom, artwork, and sidebars; from an evangelical perspective Zondervan is publishing *The NIV Life Application Commentary* series, and Broadman and Holman is producing *The New American Commentary* "for the minister or Bible student who wants to understand and expound the Scriptures," and the *Holman Old (and New) Testament Commentary* series, edited by Max Anders, a pastor.

[3]*The New Interpreter's Bible,* vol. 1 (1994), xvii.

[4]See, for instance, James Luther Mays, *Psalms,* Interpretation: A Bible Commentary for Teaching and Preaching (Louisville: Westminster John Knox Press, 1994).

[5]Among the most active in this regard have been Elizabeth Achtemeier, Ronald J. Allen, David L. Bartlett, Fred B. Craddock, John Holbert, Gail O'Day, Thomas G. Long, and Stephen Farris.

[6]D. Moody Smith, *Interpreting the Gospels for Preaching* (Philadelphia: Fortress Press, 1980), 18.

[7]Ibid., 20.

[8]Ibid., 20–21.

[9]David J. Ourisman, *From Gospel to Sermon: Preaching Synoptic Texts* (St. Louis: Chalice Press, 2000).

[10]John Holbert, *Preaching Job* (St. Louis: Chalice Press, 2000).

[11]Ibid., 162.

[12]Ronald J. Allen, *Preaching Luke-Acts* (St. Louis: Chalice Press, 2000). Other volumes in the Chalice Press *Preaching Classic Texts* series are A. Carter Shelley, *Preaching Genesis 12–36* (2001); Susan K. Hedahl and Richard P. Carlson, *Preaching 1 Corinthians 13* (St. Louis: Chalice Press, 2001); Larry Paul Jones and Jerry L. Sumney, *Preaching Apocalyptic Texts* (1999); O. Wesley Allen Jr., *Preaching Resurrection* (2000); Joseph R. Jeter Jr., *Preaching Judges* (2003); William R. Baker and Tom Ellsworth, *Preaching James* (2004); and Bruce Shields, *Preaching Romans* (2004). Abingdon's new The Great Texts commentary series includes John Holbert, *The Ten Commandments: A Preaching Commentary* (Nashville: Abingdon Press, 2002) and Stephen Farris, *Grace: A Preaching Commentary* (2003). Meanwhile David Fleer and David Bland are editing an ACU Press series: *Preaching Romans* (Abilene, Tex.: ACU Press, 2002); *Preaching Autobiography: Connecting the World of the Preacher and the World of the Text* (2001); *Preaching Luke/Acts* (2000). See also Keith Nickle, *Preaching the Gospel of Luke: Proclaiming God's Royal Rule* (Louisville: Westminster John Knox Press, 2000).

[13]David Schnasa Jacobsen and Günter Wasserberg, *Preaching Luke-Acts* (Nashville: Abingdon Press, 2001).

[14]Cornish R. Rogers and Joseph R. Jeter Jr., eds., *Preaching Through the Apocalypse* (St. Louis: Chalice Press, 1992), 15.

¹⁵Ibid., 25.

¹⁶Augustine, *On Christian Doctrine*, trans. D.W. Robertson Jr., The Library of Liberal Arts (Upper Saddle River, N. J.: Prentice Hall, 1958) III:5;7 84.

¹⁷Thomas G. Long, "The Preacher and the Beast," in *Intersections: Post-Critical Studies in Preaching*, ed. Richard L. Eslinger (Grand Rapids: William B. Eerdmans Publishing Company, 1994), 1–22. L. Susan Bond, "Apocalyptic Vocation and Liberation: The Foolish Church in the World" in *Preaching as a Theological Task: Word, Gospel, Scripture*, ed. Thomas G. Long and Edward Farley (Louisville: Westminster John Knox Press, 1996), 150–64.

¹⁸Larry Paul Jones and Jerry L. Sumney, *Preaching Apocalyptic Texts* (St. Louis: Chalice Press, 1999), 29. See 27–41.

¹⁹Ibid., 41–42.

²⁰David Schnasa Jacobsen, *Preaching in the New Creation: The Promise of New Testament Apocalyptic Texts* (Louisville: Westminster John Knox, 1999), 53–104.

²¹Kendell H. Easley, *Revelation,* Holman New Testament Commentary, ed. Max Anders (Nashville: Broadman and Holman, 1998) has provided an exegetical commentary with many features designed particularly for preachers.

²²Alyce M. McKenzie, *Preaching Proverbs: Wisdom for the Pulpit* (Louisville: Westminster John Knox, 1996) and *Preaching Biblical Wisdom in a Self-Help Society* (Nashville: Abingdon Press, 2002). See also Alyce M. McKenzie, "Out of Character! Preaching Biblical Wisdom in a Secular Age," *Journal for Preachers* 22, no.4 (1999): 44–50.

²³McKenzie, *Preaching Biblical Wisdom,* 47.

²⁴McKenzie, *Preaching Proverbs,* 20; McKenzie, *Preaching Biblical Wisdom,* 94.

²⁵McKenzie, *Preaching Proverbs,* 24.

²⁶McKenzie, *Preaching Biblical Wisdom,* 46–47.

²⁷Ibid., 101–49.

²⁸Elizabeth Achtemeier, *Preaching from the Minor Prophets* (Grand Rapids: William B. Eerdmans, 1998).

²⁹Joseph R. Jeter Jr., *Preaching Judges* (St. Louis: Chalice Press, 2003); for exegetical help with connections to modern living see also K. Lawson Younger Jr., *Judges/Ruth,* The NIV Application Commentary (Grand Rapids: Zondervan, 2002).

³⁰Robert Stephen Reid, *Preaching Mark* (St. Louis: Chalice Press, 1999).

³¹Richard A. Jensen, *Preaching Matthew's Gospel* (Lima, Ohio: CSS Publishing Company, Inc., 1998); *Preaching Mark's Gospel* (Lima, Ohio: CSS Publishing Company, Inc., 1996); *Preaching Luke's Gospel* (Lima, Ohio: CSS Publishing Company, Inc., 1997).

³²Hans Frei, *Eclipse of the Biblical Narrative* (New Haven, Conn.: Yale University Press, 1974).

³³Jack D. Kingsbury, *Matthew as Story* (Minneapolis: Augsburg/Fortress Press, 2d ed., 1988).

³⁴Richard A. Jensen, *Preaching Luke's Gospel,* 17.

³⁵Ibid., 17. See: Robert Alter, *The Art of Biblical Narrative* (London: G. Allen & Unwin, 1981) and *The World of Biblical Literature* (New York: Basic Books, 1992).

³⁶Jensen, *Preaching Luke's Gospel,* 232.

³⁷Nancy Lamers Gross, *If You Cannot Preach Like Paul...* (Grand Rapids: William B. Eerdmans, 2002), 12. She may be building here on Fred Craddock's notion of "what the text does" and Thomas Long's notion of a function statement as discussed in chapter 1.

³⁸Ibid., 37.

³⁹Ibid., 139. Her suggestion sounds akin to what James M. Robinson claimed of Barth's revolutionary commentary on Romans, in which Barth took Paul's language and "radically translated [it] and proclaimed [it] anew in the language of our day." See James M. Robinson, "Hermeneutic Since Barth," *New Frontiers in Theology,* vol. 2, ed. James M. Robinson and John Cobb Jr. (New York: Harper and Row, 1964), 6–7.

⁴⁰Gross, *If You Cannot Preach,* 125.

⁴¹Her view of homiletics as the last stage of a continuing process of hermeneutics is nonetheless still sequential; this problem is avoided if homiletics is conceived as a

parallel task to exegesis and hermeneutics. In such a model biblical criticism, both historical and literary, would proceed intermittently alongside theological criticism and homiletical criticism on parallel tracks. See Paul Scott Wilson, *God Sense: Reading the Bible for Preaching* (Nashville: Abingdon Press, 2001), 161–62.

[42]Gross, *If You Cannot Preach,* 74–76, 83.

[43]Ibid., 114–15.

[44]Edward Farley, "Preaching the Bible and Gospel," *Theology Today* 51:1 (April 1994): 90–104; and "Toward a New Paradigm for Preaching" in Long and Farley, *Preaching as a Theological Task,* 165–75,

[45]Farley, "Preaching the Bible and Gospel," 101.

[46]Karl Barth, *Church Dogmatics,* trans. G. T. Thompson (Edinburgh: T. & T. Clark, 1969 [1936]), I: 1, 127.

[47]Lucy Lind Hogan, "Rethinking Persuasion: Developing an Incarnational Theology of Preaching," *Homiletic,* 24, no. 2 (Winter 1999): 1–12; and Richard Lischer, "Why I Am Not Persuasive," *Homiletic,* 24, no.2 (Winter 1999): 13–16.

[48]See James M. Robinson, "Hermeneutic Since Barth," *New Frontiers in Theology,* vol. 2, 23–24.

Chapter 4: Theology of Preaching

[1]Martin Luther, *A Brief Instruction on What to Look for and Expect in the Gospels,* trans. E. Theodore Bachmann, *Luther's Works,* Vol. 35, ed. E. Theodore Bachmann and Helmut Lehmann (Philadelphia: Fortress Press, 1960 [1521]), 123.

[2]John Donne, *The Sermons of John Donne,* ed. Evelyn M. Simpson and George R. Potter, 10 vols. (Berkeley: University of California Press, 1953–62), 9, 127–28.

[3]Henry Ward Beecher, *Lectures on Preaching* (London; Edinburgh: T. Nelson and Sons, 1872), 127.

[4]Karl Barth, *Church Dogmatics,* trans. G. T. Thompson (Edinburgh, Scotland: T. & T. Clark, 1936), I: 1: 98–135.

[5]Ibid., 106.

[6]Ibid., 127.

[7]Ibid., 131.

[8]Karl Barth, *The Epistle to the Romans,* 6th edition, trans. Edwyn C. Hoskyns (Oxford: Oxford University Press, 1975 [1933]), 10. W. E. Sangster expressed the same thing in *The Craft of the Sermon* (London: The Epworth Press, 1954), 25. He said the Bible "tells, as no other book does…the story of God's dealing with man, and man's experience of God."

[9]David Buttrick, *A Captive Voice: The Liberation of Preaching* (Louisville: Westminster John Knox Press, 1994), 8.

[10]Ibid., 11.

[11]Ibid.

[12]Rudolf Bultmann, *Theology of the New Testament,* vols. 1 & 2, trans. Kendrick Grobel (New York: Charles Scribner's Sons, 1951 [German, 1948]), 288–292; this is part of a discussion of grace in Paul, 288–306.

[13]Ibid., 288.

[14]Ibid., 289.

[15]Ibid., 302.

[16]Gerhard Ebeling, "Word of God and Hermeneutics," in *Word and Faith* (Philadelphia: Fortress Press, 1963), 326.

[17]Gerhard Ebeling, *The Nature of Faith* (Philadelphia: Fortress Press, 1967), 331.

[18]Donald L. Miller, *Fire in Thy Mouth* (Nashville: Abingdon Press, 1954).

[19]Donald L. Miller, *The Way to Biblical Preaching* (Nashville: Abingdon Press, 1957), 13.

[20]Ibid., 15.

[21]Ibid., 16.

[22]Ibid., 24.

[23]See Henry Sloane Coffin, *Communion Through Preaching: The Monstrance of the Gospel* (New York: Charles Scribner's Sons, 1952). Coffin writes, "in His preached Word, he is both speaker and Message," (1); Jean-Jacques von Allmen, *Preaching and Congregation*, trans. B.L. Nicholas (London: Butterworth Press, 1962), argues "[Preaching is] *by* God rather than speech *about* God," (7).

[24]I. A. Richards, *Philosophy of Rhetoric* (New York: Oxford University Press, 1965 [1936]), 9–11.

[25]Ibid., 118

[26]J. L. Austin, *How to Do Things with Words: The William James Lectures at Harvard University in 1955* (Cambridge, Mass.: Harvard University Press, 1962), 6.

[27]James M. Robinson and John B. Cobb Jr., eds., *New Frontiers in Theology*, vol. 2 of *The New Hermeneutic* (New York, Evanston, London: Harper & Row, 1964).

[28]Paul Scherer, *The Word of God Sent* (Grand Rapids: Baker Book House, 1965), 24. See also Robert H. Mounce, *The Essential Nature of New Testament Preaching* (Grand Rapids: Eerdmans Press, 1960), 158.

[29]Ibid., 24.

[30]Ibid., 23.

[31]Ibid., 26; see also 23–31.

[32]David Randolph, *The Renewal of Preaching* (Philadelphia: Fortress Press, 1969), 22–23.

[33]Charles L. Rice, *Imagination and Interpretation: The Preacher and Contemporary Literature*. The Preacher's Paperback Library (Philadelphia, Fortress Press, 1970), 13–15.

[34]Lucy Atkinson Rose, *Sharing the Word: Preaching in the Roundtable Church* (Louisville: Westminster John Knox, 1997), esp., 40–41, 49–50, 60–61, 67–71; Paul Scott Wilson, *The Practice of Preaching* (Nashville: Abingdon Press, 1995), 24–25; see also the entire chapter, "Preaching as God's Event," 20–35.

[35]Rose, *Sharing the Word,* 49.

[36]Ibid.

[37]Ibid., 83.

[38]Richard Lischer, *A Theology of the Gospel: The Dynamics of the Gospel*, reprinted revised edition (Eugene, Oregon: Wipf and Stock Publishers, 2001 [1992, 1981]), 85.

[39]Ibid.

[40]Ibid.

[41]Ibid.

[42]Ibid., 88.

[43]Richard A. Jensen, *Thinking in Story: Preaching in a Post-literate Age* (Lima, Ohio: CSS, 1993), 75.

[44]Rose, *Sharing the Word*; see also, David M. Brown, *Transformational Preaching: Theory and Practice* (Lanham, Md: University Press of America, 2003).

[45]Rose, *Sharing the Word,* 59.

[46]Sangster, *Craft of the Sermon,* 16.

[47]Lischer, *Theology of the Gospel,* 88.

[48]Rose, *Sharing the Word,* 60–62. For a fuller understanding of Rose's proposal, see the charts on pages 147–49 of this book.

[49]Ibid., 60.

[50]Ibid.

[51]John Stott, *I Believe in Preaching* (London: Hodder & Stoughton, 1983), 103.

[52]Gerhard O. Forde, *Theology Is for Proclamation* (Philadelphia: Fortress, 1990), 2.

[53]Ibid.

[54]Ibid., 3.

[55]Jensen, *Thinking in Story,* 73.

[56]Richard A. Jensen, *Telling the Story: Variety and Imagination in Preaching* (Minneapolis: Augsburg Publishing House, 1980), 88–89. Eugene Lowry says that, ideally, preaching evokes the proclamation, since no preacher has possession of the Word. Thus, Lowry might not be confident in doing what Forde and Jensen suggest.

See Eugene L. Lowry, *The Sermon: Dancing the Edge of Mystery* (Nashville: Abingdon Press, 1997), 37.

[57]Jensen, *Telling the Story*, pp. 131–32.

[58]H. Grady Davis, *Design for Preaching* (Philadelphia: Fortress Press, 1958).

[59]Fred Craddock, *As One Without Authority*, revised edition (St. Louis: Chalice Press, 2001 [1971]).

[60]See for example, Horace Bushnell, *Sermons on Living Subjects* (New York: Charles Scribner's Sons, 1897); F. W. Robertson, *Sermons Preached at Brighton* (New York: Dutton, 1883).

[61]I. A. Richards, *Principles of Literary Criticism* (New York: Harcourt Brace, 1921) and *Coleridge on Imagination* (London, England: K. Paul, Trench, Trubner, 1934).

[62]Davis, *Design for Preaching*, 99.

[63]Ibid., 162.

[64]Ibid., 15.

[65]Ibid., 162.

[66]Ibid., 110–11.

[67]Ibid., 41–57.

[68]Ibid., 15.

[69]Ibid., 28–29, 49–52, 103–105.

[70]Ibid., 157–62.

[71]Ibid., 157.

[72]Ibid., 163–64.

[73]Sangster, *Craft of the Sermon*.

Chapter 5: Theological Structure I

[1]Augustine, *On the Spirit and the Letter*, (London: SPCK, 1925), ch. 6.

[2]Sidney Greidanus provides a good discussion of Luther on law and gospel in his *Preaching Christ from the Old Testament: A Contemporary Hermeneutical Method* (Grand Rapids: William B. Eerdmans, 1999), 116–26. He incorrectly assumes that Luther prescribed a law to gospel form (126).

[3]Martin Luther, "Sermons I," in *Luther's Works*, ed. and trans. John W. Doberstein, vol. 51 (Philadelphia: Muhlenburg Press, 1959), 279–80.

[4]William Perkins, *The Art of Prophesying*, Puritan Paperbacks ed. (Edinburgh & Carlisle, Pa.: The Banner of Truth Trust, 1996), 54.

[5]Ibid.

[6]John Wesley, "Letter on Preaching Christ, December 20, 1751," in *The Company of Preachers: Wisdom on Preaching, Augustine to the Present*, ed. Richard Lischer (Grand Rapids, Mich.; and Cambridge, U.K.: William B. Eerdmans, 2002), 131.

[7]Ibid., 129.

[8]See Paul Scott Wilson, "Wesley's Homiletic: Law and Gospel for Preaching," *Toronto Journal of Theology* 10, no. 2 (Fall 1994): 215–25.

[9]C. F. W. Walthers, *The Proper Distinction Between Law and Gospel*, trans. Herbert J. A. Bouman (St. Louis: Concordia, 1981 [German, 1897]).

[10]Ibid., 17.

[11]Ibid., 16.

[12]Ibid., 15.

[13]Ibid., 20.

[14]Ibid., 23.

[15]Ibid., 39.

[16]Ibid., 27.

[17]Ibid., 30.

[18]Ibid., 39–40.

[19]C. H. Spurgeon, *Lectures to My Students*, complete and unabridged (Grand Rapids: Zondervan, 1954), 70.

[20]Johann Michael Reu, *Homiletics*, trans. Albert Steinhaeuser (Grand Rapids: Baker Book House, 1967 [1922]), 141, 147–48, 156, 158.

[21]Ibid., 438.

[22]Ibid., 143.

[23]Ibid.

[24]Ibid., 140–41.

[25]Ibid., 143. This is a theme of Walthers, *Proper Distinction*, 64.

[26]Reu, *Homiletics*, 420.

[27]Walthers, *Proper Distinction*, 62. He gives examples of what violates gospel.

[28]Reu, *Homiletics*, 154.

[29] See, for example, Walter R. Bouman, "Law and Gospel," in *Concise Encyclopedia of Preaching*, ed. William H. Willimon and Richard Lischer (Louisville: Westminster John Knox Press, 1995), 298–300, esp. 299.

[30]See Will Herberg, "Introduction–The Social Philosophy of Karl Barth" in Karl Barth, *Community State and Church*, trans. Will Herberg (Gloucester, Mass.: Peter Smith, 1968), 41–43.

[31]Karl Barth, "Gospel and Law," in *Community State and Church*, 80.

[32]H. H. Farmer, *The Servant of the Word* (Philadelphia: Fortress Press, 1965 [1942]), 44–45.

[33]Ibid., 45.

[34]Ibid., 46.

[35]Ibid.

[36]Ibid., 48.

[37]Ibid., 49.

[38]Morris J. Niedenthal, "The Irony and Grammar of the Gospel," in Edmund A. Steimle, Morris J. Niedenthal, and Charles L. Rice, *Preaching the Story* (Philadelphia: Fortress Press, 1980), 142; see 141–50.

[39]Ibid., 148.

[40]Ibid., 149.

[41]H. Grady Davis, *Design for Preaching* (Philadelphia: Fortress Press, 1958), 231.

[42]Ibid., 49.

[43]Richard R. Caemmerer, *Preaching for the Church* (St. Louis: Concordia, 1959), 25.

[44]Ibid.

[45]Ibid., 27.

[46]Ibid., 15–20.

[47]Ibid., 21–26.

[48]Ibid., 88.

[49]Ibid., 96.

[50]Ibid., 27–33, 89–90.

[51]Ibid., 35–39.

[52]Ibid., 96.

[53]Ibid., 79–111.

[54]Ibid., 97.

[55]Ibid., 177–214.

[56]See Fred B. Craddock, "The Gospel of God," in *Preaching as a Theological Venture: Word, Gospel, Scripture,* ed. Thomas G. Long and Edward Farley (Louisville: Westminster John Knox Press, 1996), 73–82.

[57]I have this from conversation with Charles L. Rice who is working on a book on Steimle's preaching. Concerning Farmer and Steimle, see also Niedenthal, "Irony and Grammar," 142.

[58]See Charles L. Rice, "Theology, Liturgy, and the Popular Preacher: Edmund A Steimle on 'The Protestant Hour,' 1963–74," *Papers of the Annual Meeting of the Academy of Homiletics* (n.p.: The Academy of Homiletics, 1994), 123–33; and Thomas G. Long, "Edmund Steimle and the Shape of Contemporary Homiletics," *Princeton Seminary Bulletin*, 11, no. 3 (New Series 1990): 253–67, esp. 260–63. Long attributes to Steimle a sermon movement of law to gospel, but this may be a result of reading current theory back into Steimle; a comprehensive study of Steimle's notes and sermons may be needed to substantiate Long's claim.

[59]Herman G. Stuempfle Jr., *Preaching Law and Gospel* (Philadelphia: Fortress Press, 1978), 23–32.

[60]Ibid., 47–61.
[61]Ibid., 78.
[62]Ibid., 79.
[63]Ibid., 48–58.
[64]Ibid., 62–75.
[65]Ibid., 77.
[66]Ibid., 76.
[67]See Stuempfle's acknowledgment of the public sector, 72–74.
[68]Fred B. Craddock, *As One Without Authority,* rev. ed. (St. Louis: Chalice Press, 2001).
[69]Milton Crum Jr., *Manual on Preaching: A New Process of Sermon Development* (Valley Forge, Pa.: Judson Press, 1977), 76.
[70]Ibid., 76–81.
[71]Ibid., 19–21, 80–81.
[72]Ibid., 76.
[73]Ibid., 20
[74]Ibid., 78.
[75]Ibid., 21. Italics my own.
[76]See especially the sketch in ibid., 80.

Chapter 6: Theological Structure II

[1]Milton Crum Jr., *Manual on Preaching: A New Process of Sermon Development* (Valley Forge, Pa.: Judson Press, 1977).
[2]Robert Scholes and Robert Kellogg, *The Nature of Narrative* (New York: Oxford University Press, 1966), 212.
[3]Frederick Buechner, *Telling the Truth, The Gospel as Tragedy, Comedy and Fairy Tale* (New York: Harper & Row, 1977), 7. Eugene Lowry cites Buechner on page 49 of *The Homiletical Plot: The Sermon as Narrative Art Form* (Atlanta: John Knox Press, 1980).
[4]Buechner, *Telling the Truth,* 7.
[5]Lowry, *Homiletical Plot,* 29.
[6]Ibid., 38.
[7]Reversal is constituted by "a *radical discontinuity* between the gospel and worldly wisdom," ibid., 60.
[8]Crum, *Manual on Preaching,* 52–86, 111–16.
[9]Lowry, *Homiletical Plot,* 48.
[10]Ibid., 56.
[11]Eugene L. Lowry, *The Sermon: Dancing the Edge of Mystery.* (Nashville: Abingdon Press, 1997), 78.
[12]Ibid., 28.
[13]Ibid., 36–37, 52–53.
[14]Ibid., 47.
[15]See Richard L. Eslinger, *The Web of Preaching: New Options in Homiletic Method* (Nashville: Abingdon Press, 2002), 51–52, 237–38.
[16]Richard Lischer, *A Theology of Preaching: The Dynamics of the Gospel,* Abingdon Preacher's Library, ed. William D. Thompson (Nashville: Abingdon Press, 1981), 50.
[17]Crum, *Manual on Preaching,* 19.
[18]Lischer, *A Theology,* 50.
[19]Ibid.
[20]Ibid., 52.
[21]Ibid., 56.
[22]Ibid., 63.
[23]Ibid., 64.
[24]Ibid., 49; see 48–50.

²⁵Ibid., 49–50.

²⁶Paul Scott Wilson, *Imagination of the Heart: New Understandings in Preaching* (Nashville: Abingdon Press, 1988).

²⁷I. A. Richards, *Coleridge on Imagination,* ed. John Constable (New York: Routledge, 2001).

²⁸C. F. W. Walthers, *The Proper Distinction Between Law and Gospel,* trans. Herbert J. A. Bouman (St. Louis: Concordia, 1981 [German, 1897], 28.

²⁹When David Buttrick talks about moves or individual paragraphs that bring a "statement of a move" into "focus" (Buttrick, *Homiletic: Moves and Structures* [Philadelphia: Fortress Press, 1987], 37) within the first three sentences–for example, "We are sinners" (p. 28)–I understand him to be talking about how concerns of the text and of the sermon actually function in preaching. They help students to develop appropriate links between the Bible and now, links that are plain and the congregation can follow.

³⁰Wilson, *The Practice of Preaching* (Nashville: Abingdon Press, 1995).

³¹Wilson, *The Four Pages of the Sermon: A Guide to Biblical Preaching* (Nashville: Abingdon Press, 1999).

³²Stephen Farris, "Preaching Law as Gospel: Some Reflections on and from Psalm 119," *Papers of the Annual Meeting of the Academy of Homiletics* (n.p.: The Academy of Homiletics, 1998), pagination not provided.

³³Stephen Farris, *Grace: A Preaching Commentary* (Nashville: Abingdon Press, 2003).

³⁴Crum, *Manual on Preaching,* 80.

³⁵Ibid., Crum, 76.

³⁶Ibid., Crum, 80. In a concluding chapter to my *The Four Pages of the Sermon* I talk about various possibilities for reshuffling the pages, pp. 243–251. Foster McCurley offers a 1996 variation, although McCurley does not focus on grace: Introduction, Situation Now, Situation Then, What God Is Doing Then, and What God Is Doing Now. See: Foster R. McCurley, *Wrestling with the Word: Preaching from the Hebrew Bible* (Valley Forge, Pa.: Trinity Press International, 1996), 195.

³⁷Ronald J. Allen, ed., *Patterns of Preaching: A Sermon Sampler* (St. Louis: Chalice Press, 1998), 80–87; Mark Barger Elliott, *Creative Styles of Preaching* (Louisville: Westminster John Knox Press, 2000), 77–83; Richard L. Eslinger, *The Web Of Preaching: New Options in Homiletic Method* (Nashville: Abingdon Press, 2002), 201–245.

³⁸L. Susan Bond makes this comment and attributes it also to David Buttrick in her "Taming the Parable: The Problem of Parable as Substitute Myth," *Papers of the Annual Meeting of the Academy of Homiletics* (n.p.: The Academy of Homiletics, 1999), 6.

Chapter 7: Variations and Alternative Theologies of Preaching

¹Bryan Chapell, *Christ-Centered Preaching: Redeeming the Expository Sermon* (Grand Rapids: Baker Books, 1994), 12.

²Ibid., 47.

³Ibid., 289.

⁴Ibid., 310.

⁵Ibid., 289.

⁶Ibid., 277.

⁷Ibid., 292.

⁸Ibid., 296.

⁹Ibid., 267.

¹⁰Mary Catherine Hilkert, *Naming Grace: Preaching and the Sacramental Imagination* (New York: Continuum, 1997), 25.

¹¹Ibid., 53

¹²Ibid., 31–34.

¹³Ibid., 43–38.

¹⁴Ibid., 49.

¹⁵Ibid., 94.

[16]See James F. Kay's discussion of this in relation to Bultmann in his *Christus Praesens: A Reconsideration of Rudolf Bultmann's Christology* (Grand Rapids: William. B. Eerdmans, 1994), 114.

[17]Gerhard O. Forde, *Theology Is for Proclamation* (Philadelphia: Fortress, 1990), 2.

[18]Henry H. Mitchell, *Preaching as Celebration and Experience* (Nashville: Abingdon Press, 1990), 41.

[19]Ibid., 62.

[20]James Harris, "Thesis–Antithesis–Synthesis," in *Patterns of Preaching: A Sermon Sampler,* ed. Ronald J. Allen (St. Louis: Chalice Press, 1998), 36–42.

[21]Mitchell, *Preaching as Celebration,* 57.

[22]Ibid.

[23]Ibid., 63.

[24]Frank Thomas, *They Like to Never Quit Praisin' God: The Role of Celebration in Preaching* (Cleveland, Ohio: United Church Press, 1997), 75.

[25]Mitchell, *Preaching as Celebration,* 67.

[26]Thomas, *Never Quit,* 31.

[27]Cleophus J. LaRue, *The Heart of Black Preaching* (Louisville: Westminster John Knox Press, 2000), 69.

[28]Ibid., 70.

[29]Ibid., 71.

[30]Ibid., 72–83.

[31]Charles L. Bartow, *God's Human Speech: A Practical Theology of Proclamation* (Grand Rapids: William B. Eerdmans, 1997), 28.

[32]Ibid., 38.

[33]Ibid., 35.

[34]Ibid., 111.

[35]Ibid., 121, adapted.

[36]Ibid., 128–29.

[37]Marjorie Hewitt Suchocki, *The Whispered Word: A Theology of Preaching* (St. Louis: Chalice Press, 1999), 3.

[38]Ibid., 6.

[39]Ibid., 7.

[40]Ibid., 10.

[41]Ibid.

[42]Ibid., 13.

[43]Ibid., 20.

[44]Ibid., 34.

[45]Ibid., 39.

[46]Ibid., 42.

[47]Ibid.

[48]Ibid., 42–44.

[49]Charles L. Campbell. *Preaching Jesus: New Directions for Homiletics in Hans Frei's Postliberal Theology* (Grand Rapids: William B. Eerdmans, 1997), 122–23.

[50]Ibid., 33, 38.

[51]Ibid., 56.

[52]Ibid., 45.

[53]Ibid., 39, 93, 95.

[54]Ibid., 61.

[55]Ibid., 122. George A. Lindbeck also spoke of a cognitive-propositional approach to religion that largely predates historical criticism. See his *The Nature of Doctrine: Religion and Theology in a Postliberal Age* (Louisville: The Westminster Press, 1984), 16–17.

[56]Campbell, *Preaching Jesus,* 230.

[57]Ibid., 256–57.

[58]David J. Lose, "Narrative and Proclamation in a Postliberal World," *Homiletic,* 23:1 (Summer 1998): 1–14, esp. 6–9. See also his *Confessing Jesus Christ: Preaching in a*

Postmodern World (Grand Rapids: William B. Eerdmans, 2003), 113–26. This book was not available to me in the writing of this manuscript.

[59]Forde, *Theology Is for Proclamation,* 130. See also 129–33. For another fresh perspective on preaching as atonement see Thomas F. Torrance, *Preaching Christ Today: The Gospel and Scientific Thinking* (Grand Rapids: Wm. B. Eerdmans, 1994), 32–34. Torrance stays with the substitution theory of atonement understood as the faithfulness of God in Christ, who takes our place so that we can have his, using even our sins as the means of binding us to himself.

[60]Michael Quicke, "Let Anyone with Ears to Hear, Listen," *Papers for the annual meeting of Evangelical Homiletics, 2002,* available at http://www.evangelicalhomiletics.com/Papers2002/Quicke.htm.

[61]Donald English, *An Evangelical Theology of Preaching* (Nashville: Abingdon Press, 1996), 16–17, 30.

[62]Craig A. Loscalzo, *Evangelistic Preaching that Connects: Guidance in Shaping Fresh and Appealing Sermons* (Downers Grove, Ill.: InterVarsity Press, 1995), 42.

[63]David Buttrick, *Preaching the New and the Now* (Louisville: Westminster John Knox Press, 1998), 13.

Chapter 8: Pastoral and Prophetic Homiletics

[1]Ronald J. Allen, Barbara Shires Blaisdell, and Scott Black Johnson, *Theology for Preaching: Authority, Truth, and Knowledge of God in a Postmodern Ethos* (Nashville: Abingdon Press, 1997), 42.

[2]Ibid., 44–48

[3]Ibid., 49–57.

[4]William H. Willimon, *Peculiar Speech: Preaching to the Baptized* (Grand Rapids: William B. Eerdmans, 1992), 4, 16.

[5]Ibid., 56.

[6]William H. Willimon, *The Intrusive Word: Preaching to the Unbaptized* (Grand Rapids: William B. Eerdmans, 1994), 40.

[7]André Resner, *Preacher and Cross: Person and Message in Theology and Rhetoric* (Grand Rapids: William B. Eerdmans, 1999), 137.

[8]Ibid., 147.

[9]See ibid., 105–28.

[10]Ibid., 4, 148.

[11]Walter J. Burghardt, S.J., *Preaching the Just Word* (New Haven, Conn.: Yale University Press, 1996), 6.

[12]Ibid., x

[13]Ibid., 54.

[14]Ibid., 55.

[15]Ibid., 56.

[16]Ibid., 57.

[17]Ibid., 22.

[18]Ibid., 59.

[19]Stanley P. Saunders and Charles L. Campbell, *The Word on the Street: Performing the Scriptures in the Urban Context* (Grand Rapids, Mich. and Cambridge, UK: William B. Eerdmans, 2000), 89.

[20]Ibid., 85.

[21]Ibid., 104.

[22]Kathy Black, *A Healing Homiletic: Preaching and Disability* (Nashville: Abingdon Press, 1996). See also her, "A Perspective of the Disabled: Transforming Images of God, Interdependence, and Healing," in *Preaching Justice: Ethnic and Cultural Perspectives,* ed. Christine M. Smith (Cleveland: United Church Press, 1998), 6–26.

[23]Black, "Perspective of the Disabled," 7.

[24]Black, *A Healing Homiletic,* 183–86.

[25]Arthur Van Seters, *Preaching and Ethics* (St. Louis: Chalice Press, 2004).

26James M. Childs, *Preaching Justice: The Ethical Vocation of Word and Sacrament* (Harrisburg, Pa.: Trinity Press International, 2000).

27Smith, *Preaching Justice.*

28John S. McClure and Nancy J. Ramsay, eds., *Telling the Truth: Preaching about Sexual and Domestic Violence* (Cleveland: United Church Press, 1998).

29Ray John Marek, O.M.I., and Daniel E. Harris, C.M., "A Public Voice: Preaching on Justice Issues," in *Theological Education* 38, no. 1 (2001): 47–59.

30David P. Gushee and Robert H. Long, *A Bolder Pulpit: Reclaiming the Moral Dimension of Preaching* (Valley Forge, Pa.: Judson Press, 1998).

31Ibid., 43.

32Ibid., 44.

33Ibid., 48.

34Ibid., 44.

35Ibid., 46.

36Ibid., 49–53.

37John R. Bisagno, *Principle Preaching: How to Create and Deliver Purpose Driven Sermons for Life Applications* (Nashville: Broadman and Holman Publishers, 2002), 5–7.

38Ibid., 4.

39See the final chapter in Van Seters, *Preaching and Ethics.*

40Charles L. Campbell, *The Word Before the Powers: An Ethic of Preaching* (Louisville and London: Westminster John Knox Press, 2002), 93–94.

41Ibid., 70–71.

42Ibid., 79.

43Ibid., 82–23.

44See: Christine M. Smith, *Preaching as Weeping, Confession, and Resistance: Radical Responses to Radical Evil* (Louisville: Westminster John Knox Press), 1992. Campbell was also influenced in this by Barbara Patterson, "Preaching as Nonviolent Resistance," in John S. McClure and Nancy J. Ramsay, *Telling the Truth,* 99–109.

45Campbell, *Word Before the Powers,* 89, n. 2.

46Ibid., 90, n. 5.

47Ibid., 91, n. 8.

48Ibid., 103, 122.

49Ibid., 141–153.

50From an evangelical perspective, see Joe E. Trull and James E. Carter, *Ministerial Ethics* (Nashville: Broadman and Holman, 1993).

51Lucy Lind Hogan and Robert Reid, *Connecting with the Congregation: Rhetoric and the Art of Preaching* (Nashville: Abingdon Press, 1999), 47–68.

52Resner, *Preacher and Cross.*

53Campbell, *Word Before the Powers,* 158–59; see also 159–88.

54Mary Catherine Hilkert, *Naming Grace: Preaching and the Sacramental Imagination* (New York: Continuum, 1997), 144–65.

55Mary Donovan Turner and Mary Lin Hudson, *Saved from Silence: Finding Women's Voice in Preaching* (St. Louis: Chalice Press, 1999).

56Christine M. Smith, *Weaving the Sermon: Preaching from a Feminist Perspective* (Louisville: Westminster/John Knox Press, 1989).

57Carol M. Norén, *The Woman in the Pulpit* (Nashville: Abingdon Press, 1991).

58G. Lee Ramsey, Jr., *Care-full Preaching: From Sermon to Caring Community* (St. Louis: Chalice Press, 2000), 3.

59Ibid., 147–202.

60Edward P. Wimberly, *Moving from Shame to Self-Worth: Preaching and Pastoral Care* (Nashville: Abingdon Press, 1999).

61Robert C. Dykstra, *Discovering a Sermon: Personal Pastoral Preaching* (St. Louis: Chalice Press, 2001), 9.

62Ibid., 28.

63Ibid., 51–52.

64Ibid., 57.

[65]Lenora Tubbs Tisdale, *Preaching as Local Theology and Folk Art*, Fortress Resources for Preaching (Minneapolis: Fortress Press, 1997), 45.

[66]Ibid., 42.

[67]Ibid., 64–77.

[68]Ibid., 77–90.

[69]Ibid., 124.

[70]Joseph R. Jeter Jr. and Ronald J. Allen, *One Gospel, Many Ears: Preaching for Different Listeners in the Congregation* (St. Louis: Chalice Press, 2002), 128.

[71]The Greek word *perichoresis* applied to the Trinity implies "a kind of circle dance in which the persons move around the circle in a way that implies intimacy, equality, unity yet distinction, and love," ibid., 121.

[72]Ibid., 128.

[73]See chapter 9.

[74]James R. Nieman and Thomas G. Rogers, *Preaching to Every Pew: Cross-Cultural Strategies* (Minneapolis: Fortress Press, 2002), 147.

[75]Ibid., 150.

[76]Ibid., 151.

[77]Ibid., 152.

Chapter 9: Postmodern or Radical Postmodern?

[1]See Art Van Seters, *Preaching and Ethics* (St. Louis: Chalice Press, 2004).

[2]Paul Scott Wilson, "Postmodernism, Theology, and Preaching," in *Papers of the Annual Meeting of the Academy of Homiletics* (The Academy of Homiletics, 1994), 149–58, esp. 150.

[3]Ronald J. Allen, Barbara Shires Blaisdell, and Scott Black Johnson, *Theology for Preaching: Authority, Truth, and Knowledge of God in a Postmodern Ethos* (Nashville: Abingdon Press, 1997), 42. See page 120 for a discussion of this book.

[4]Robert Stephen Reid, "Postmodernism and the Function of the New Homiletic in Post-Christendom Congregations," *Homiletic* 20, no 2 (Winter, 1995): 1–13.

[5]Ibid., 10. Reid and Lucy Hogan later make this distinction between what they call the "Practical Postmodern" and the kerygmatic approaches: "they differ in the degree to which they are willing to tell what the 'redemptive' point is that is derived from the retelling of the biblical story." Lucy Lind Hogan and Robert Reid, *Connecting with the Congregation: Rhetoric and the Art of Preaching* (Nashville: Abingdon Press, 1999), 126.

[6]Reid and Hogan see the transformative and New Homiletics positions as practical postmodern, *Connecting*, 121. See also Eugene Lowry, *The Sermon: Dancing the Edge of Mystery* (Nashville: Abingdon Press, 1997), 20–28; Alyce McKenzie, "Homiletical Grammars: Retrospect and Prospects," *Homiletic* 26, no 2 (Winter 2001): 1–10, esp. 8–9; Jeffrey E. Bullock, "Preaching in a Post-Modern Wor[l]d," *Papers for the Annual Meeting of the Academy of Homiletics* (The Academy of Homiletics, 2002), 153–63; James W. Thompson, *Preaching Like Paul: Homiletical Wisdom for Today* (Louisville: Westminster John Knox Press, 2001), 7.

[7]David James Randolph first identified these features in his *The Renewal of Preaching* (Philadelphia: Fortress Press, 1969), 22–23.

[8]I am grateful to the first four of these colleagues for their patience in giving feedback to a first draft of this material; they do not endorse what I am saying but they have improved the final piece by their critique. Lucy Rose died not long after the publication of her book.

[9]See the previous discussion of Campbell in chapter 8.

[10]John S. McClure, *Other-wise Preaching* (St. Louis, Chalice Press, 2001), 47–95.

[11]The subtitle of Christine M. Smith's *Preaching as Weeping, Confession and Resistance* is *Radical Responses to Radical Evil* (Louisville: Westminster/John Knox Press, 1992). Hogan and Reid identify the postliberal paradigm as "thoroughly postmodern," *Connecting*, 121. Together with other scholars named above, I consider the last several decades in homiletics to be postmodern.

[12]See for instance, Joseph M. Webb, *Comedy and Preaching* (St. Louis: Chalice Press, 1998), a book that emphasizes the role of narrative and comedy in establishing conversational preaching.

[13]Lucy Atkinson Rose, *Sharing the Word: Preaching in the Roundtable Church* (Nashville: Abingdon Press, 1997), 123.

[14]John S. McClure, *The Roundtable Pulpit: Where Preaching and Leadership Meet* (Nashville: Abingdon Press, 1996).

[15]Webb has a significant discussion of the other in Joseph M. Webb, *Preaching and the Challenge of Pluralism* (St. Louis: Chalice Press, 1998), 112–18.

[16]This is a phrase McClure repeatedly uses without unpacking. See McClure, *Other-wise Preaching* (St. Louis: Chalice Press, 2001), 9, 10, 125, 128, 131.

[17]For a discussion of these authorities, see the chapter on authority in Van Seters, *Preaching and Ethics.*

[18]McClure, *Other-wise,* 3.

[19]Ibid., 10.

[20]Ibid., 2–4.

[21]Ibid., 7.

[22]Ibid., 19–21.

[23]Ibid., 29–30.

[24]Ibid., 30–31.

[25]Ibid., 35–37.

[26]Ibid., 39.

[27]Ibid., 43.

[28]Ibid., 44.

[29]Ibid., 29.

[30]Ibid., 45.

[31]Ibid., 3.

[32]Ibid., 72. Anna Carter Florence teaches homiletics at Columbia Seminary in Decatur, Georgia.

[33]McClure's language for this matter is "the glory of the Infinite" in a section that deals with these matters; see ibid., 123–30.

[34]See L. Susan Bond, *Trouble with Jesus: Women, Christology, and Preaching* (St. Louis: Chalice Press, 1999), 40–42.

[35]For a significant interpretation of the difference between theology from above and theology from below for preaching, see Richard Lischer, "Preaching as the Church's Language," in Gail R. O'Day and Thomas G. Long, *Listening to the Word: Studies in Honor of Fred B. Craddock* (Nashville: Abingdon Press, 1993), 121–22.

[36]Christine M. Smith, *Preaching as Weeping,* 3.

[37]Ibid., 4

[38]Christine M. Smith, *Risking the Terror: Resurrection in this Life* (Cleveland: The Pilgrim Press, 2001), 111.

[39]Ibid., 89.

[40]Ibid., 2.

[41]Ibid., 2.

[42]"We use the word *resurrection* to point to those concrete moments and experiences that are part of the reign of God," ibid., 73.

[43]Ibid., 3.

[44]Ibid., 111.

[45]Ibid., 11.

[46]McClure, *Other-wise,* 137.

[47]Ibid., 134.

[48]Ibid.

[49]Webb, *Preaching and the Challenge of Pluralism,* xii.

[50]Ibid., 58.

[51]Ibid., 59–61.

[52]Ibid., 74. He cites with approval the work of Burton L. Mack.

53Ibid., 103–4.
54Bond, *Trouble with Jesus,* 40–42; and Jon Sobrino, S.J., *Christology at the Crossroads* (Maryknoll, N.Y.: Orbis, 1984), 338–39.
55Bond, *Trouble with Jesus,* 41.
56Ibid., 181.
57Ibid.
58Ibid., 114.
59McClure, *Other-wise,* 132. See also x–xi.
60Ibid., 1.
61For example, Rose casts transformational preaching as an expression of theology from below when she says of it that "the dominant focus shifts to the human side of the encounter," and "transformational preaching emphasizes more the preacher's responsibility in the sermon's becoming an event," Rose, *Sharing the Word,* 60. She includes me in this category, 61–62, and she may be right, but not with this description.
62Lowry, *Dancing,* 31–32.
63Reid and Hogan have four categories: traditional, kerygmatic, New Homiletic, and Thoroughly Postmodern (Postliberal), *Connecting,* 121.
64Charles L. Bartow, *God's Human Speech: A Practical Theology of Proclamation* (Grand Rapids: William B. Eerdmans, 1997), 37, n. 31.
65Lenora Tubbs Tisdale, *Preaching as Local Theology and Folk Art,* Fortress Resources for Preaching (Minneapolis: Fortress Press, 1997), 43. She is drawing on David Kelsey's use of the term.
66McClure, *Roundtable Pulpit,* 14.
67McClure, *Other-wise,* 18–19.
68See for instance, John Wesley, *John Wesley's Fifty-Three Sermons,* ed. Edward H. Sugden, (Nashville: Abingdon Press, 1981).
69I discuss this at length in Paul Scott Wilson, *The Four Pages of the Sermon: A Guide to Biblical Preaching* (Nashville: Abingdon Press, 1999), 73–129.
70See these categories in Van Seters, *Preaching and Ethics.*
71See Paul Scott Wilson, *God Sense: Reading the Bible for Preaching,* (Nashville: Abingdon Press, 2001). esp. 9–22, 91–111.
72Wilson, *God Sense,* 104–5.

INDEX OF NAMES AND SUBJECTS

prophetic homiletics, 119
prophets, 47
Proverbs, 46–47,
Puritan plain style, 21, 98

Q

Quicke, Michael, 114

R

radical postmodern, 2, 135–58
Rahner, Karl, 104
Ramsay, Nancy J., 125
Ramsey, G. Lee, 129–30
Randolph, David, 64
reader response, 2, 157
Reid, Robert Stephen, 48, 129, 136
resistance, preaching as, 127–29
Resner, André, 121–22, 129
resolution, 85, 88, 89, 97
Reu, Johann Michael, 9, 19, 21, 27, 78–79
revelation, 2, 51, 60, 64
Revelation, book of, 44–45
reversal, 89, 170 n. 7
reverse-*ethos*, 122
rhetoric, 12, 28, 37, 42, 48, 121
    theme sentence, 9
Rice, Charles L., 30, 36, 64, 88, 169 n. 57, n. 58
Richards, I. A., 63, 70, 92
Ricoeur, Paul, 27, 29, 50, 140
Riegert, Eduard, R., 162 n. 37, 163 n. 40
Robertson, F. W., 69
Robinson, Haddon, 10, 15
Robinson, James M., 165 n. 39
Rogers, Cornish R., 44
Rogers, Thomas, 133–34
Romantics, 63, 69–70
Rose, Lucy, 19, 65–67, 137, 146–49
roundtable, 18–19, 138

S

sacramental imagination, 103–5
sacraments, 60
Sangster, W. E., 66, 72
Saunders, Stanley, P., 123–24
Scherer, Paul, 64
Schillebeeckx, Edward, 104
Scholes, Robert, 87
scripture,
    authors, human, 29
    authority of, 23, 27, 53
    doctrine of, 51
    God sense of, 12, 156
    literal meaning of, 45, 112, 155
    moral sense of, 154–55
    objective meaning of, 26, 39
    revelation, as, 2, 7, 140
self-worth, 130
sermon form, *see* form.
sermon goals, 99–100
shame, 130
Shelley, A. Carter, 164 n. 12
Shields, Bruce E., 37
sin, corporate, 82
situation, 85, 88, 97
Smith, Christine, M., 125, 127, 129, 131, 137, 141
Smith, D. Moody, 42
Society for Biblical Literature, 161 n. 1
Spurgeon, C. H., 78
Steck, Hans Odil, 161 n. 7
Steimle, Edmund, 36, 88
Stokes, Karen, 163 n. 39
Stott, John, 67
Stuempfle, Herman G., 83–84, 90, 91, 95
substitution theory of language, 145
Suchocki, Marjorie Hewitt, 101, 110–12, 114
Sumney, Jerry L., 45, 164 n. 12

Sweeney, Marvin A., 161 n. 7
symbolic interaction theory, 143
symbols, hub, 143

T

Taylor, Gardner, 36
Taylor, James C., 14
theme horizon, 14
theme sentence, 9–24
    God and, 95
theological anthropology, 139
theological interpretation,
    32–33, 35, 54
theology, 59–115
    Christus Victor, 142
    metaphor, as, 143
    sermon form and, 73–101
Thomas, Frank, 107
Thompson, James W., 136
Thompson, William D., 161 n.
    12
Tisdale, Lenora Tubbs, 131–32
Torrance, James B., 114
Torrance, Thomas F., 173 n. 59
transcendence, 141
transformative preaching,
    66–69, 104, 106, 128
Troeger, Thomas, 36, 161 n. 52,
    162 n. 37, 163 n. 40
trouble, 87–100
    critique of, 97–98
    defined, 94
trouble/ grace school, 87, 100,
    115, 130, 153, 156
Trinity, 12, 111, 133
Tuckett, Christopher, 161 n. 7
Turner, Mary Donovan, 129

V

Van Seters, Arthur, 125, 163 n.
    53
Von Allmen, Jean-Jacques, 167
    n. 23

Von Rad, Gerhard, 37, 157

W

Wallace, James A., 162 n. 37
Walthers, C. F. W., 76–78, 93
Wardlaw, Donald M., 27, 36
Warren, Timothy S., 159 n. 6
Wasserberg, Günter, 44
Webb, Joseph M., 137, 139,
    143–44, 151
Wesley, John, 75–76, 153
White, Richard, 161 n. 12, 163
    n. 54
Whitehead, Alfred North, 143
Williamson, Clark M., 162 n.15
Willimon, William, 121
Wilson, Paul Scott, 15, 24,
    91–97, 162 n. 37, 167 n. 34
Wimberly, Edward P., 130
Winnicott, D. W., 131
wisdom, 46
women in ministry, 129
Word of God, 7, 8, 29, 51, 54,
    60, 61, 63, 65, 68–69, 75,
    103, 111–12, 124, 151, 156
word whispered, 110
Wordsworth, William, 69
Wright, Jeremiah, 107

Z

Zacchaeus, 123
Zvi, Ehud Ben, 161 n. 7